Never Quit

Never Quit

How One Man Overcame Adversity to Become America's Greatest Miler

Glenn Cunningham

Edited by Robert B. Gregg
With Cindy Cunningham
Foreword by Jim Ryun

University Press of Kansas

Published by the University Press of Kansas (Lawrence, Kansas 66045), which was organized by the Kansas Board of Regents and is operated and funded by Emporia State University, Fort Hays State University, Kansas State University, Pittsburg State University, the University of Kansas, and Wichita State University.

Library of Congress Cataloging-in-Publication Data
Names: Cunningham, Glenn, 1909–1988, author. | Gregg, Robert B. editor | Cunningham, Cindy editor
Title: Never quit : how one man overcame adversity to become America's greatest miler / Glenn Cunningham ; edited by Robert B. Gregg with Cindy Cunningham ; foreword by Jim Ryun.
Identifiers: LCCN 2024060689 (print) | LCCN 2024060690 (ebook) | ISBN 9780700638918 (paperback) | ISBN 9780700638925 (ebook)
Subjects: LCSH: Cunningham, Glenn, 1909–1988. | Runners (Sports)—United States—Biography. | Burns and scalds—Patients—United States—Biography. | Kansas—Biography. | BISAC: BIOGRAPHY & AUTOBIOGRAPHY / Sports | SPORTS & RECREATION / Olympics & Paralympics | LCGFT: Autobiographies
Classification: LCC GV1061.15.C86 A3 2025 (print) | LCC GV1061.15.C86 (ebook) | DDC 796.42092 [B] —dc23/eng/20250218
LC record available at https://lccn.loc.gov/2024060689.
LC ebook record available at https://lccn.loc.gov/2024060690.

British Library Cataloguing-in-Publication Data is available.
Authorised Representative Details: Easy Access System Europe
Mustamäe tee 50, 10621 Tallinn, Estonia, gpsr.requests@easproject.com

Printed in the United States of America

10 9 8 7 6 5 4 3 2 1

The paper used in this publication is acid free and meets the minimum requirements of the American National Standard for Permanence of Paper for Printed Library Materials Z39.48–1992.

To young people everywhere who dream of success:
You will never reach any higher than you aim,
so set your goals high, then
endeavor to reach them with honor and integrity . . .
and never give up.
—Glenn Cunningham

Success is failure turned inside out—
the silver tint of the clouds of doubt,
and when you never can tell how close you are,
it may be near when it seems afar;
so stick to the fight when you're hardest hit—
it's when things seem worst,
you must not quit.
—Edgar Albert Guest, "Don't Quit"

But seek ye first the kingdom of God, and his righteousness; and all these things shall be added unto you.
—Matthew 6:33

Contents

Foreword by Jim Ryun

It was April of 1981, a month that historically had been the month of the relay meets at Texas, Kansas, and Drake. These had been the spring testing grounds, prepping me for the big summer meets and international competition as a runner. Over the years, I had anchored my Kansas teams to many victories in the 4 x mile, the 2-mile relay, the sprint medley, and the distance medley relay.

However, on this day at the Kansas Relays, I wasn't competing. As my thirty-fourth birthday approached, my best days were behind me, and I was slowly jogging a lap of honor with two other great Kansas milers.

Inside of me, Wes Santee had the same upright stride he'd always had, which had almost carried him to the first sub-4-minute mile in history. He even had the same flattop crew cut. Inside of him, small, a little hunched over, and heavier around the middle, was the man whose shoulders we had both stood on, the first great Kansas miler and the first Kansan to hold the world record in the mile, running a scintillating 4:04 mile indoors in 1938. Every Kansas schoolboy knew of Glenn Cunningham.

We'd read about him in elementary school. Glenn Cunningham, the "Iron Horse of Kansas" and the "Elkhart Express," captured the imagination of many, not just for his incredible feats on the track but also for what he had overcome to get there. After he was severely burned in a fire that killed his brother, the doctors thought he would never walk again, much less run. But run he did, making two Olympic teams and setting world records in the 800 meters, the 1500 meters, and the mile, indoors and outdoors.

After his running career ended, Glenn developed a youth ranch in Augusta, Kansas, about thirty minutes from my childhood home. He

Jim Ryun receives the Presidential Medal of Freedom from President Donald Trump, 2020.

used this opportunity not to grow his reputation but rather to help troubled youth.

I first met him during the summer of 1965 when he had driven over from Augusta to visit Wichita East High. Years later, I discovered that he'd come to see the gangly teenager who had already set 3:59 for the mile and made an Olympic team. My coach, Bob Timmons, spotted Glenn quietly standing next to the track watching my workout. "Jim, come over here. I want you to meet someone." I don't recall the details of the conversation. However, I do remember this humble man interacting with a quiet and shy teenage boy who was starstruck at meeting this man who had accomplished so much.

As we finished our lap of honor on that spring day in April, I turned to Glenn and began chatting about the many memories we shared as two Kansans who had previously held the world mile record.

As we talked, I noted that Glenn was in some pain from our jog, although he wasn't complaining. With some prodding, he said that his legs ached. They'd never really stopped hurting from the fire all those years before. I was stunned.

Running is a difficult sport. Being a miler is another thing altogether. To become a great miler takes an incredible amount of work, blending speed and strength. Glenn had accomplished all that work with legs that were in constant pain. Glenn passed away a few short years later, but his courage lives on.

As time passed, I realized that Glenn's strength came from his deep Christian faith. His favorite Bible verse was Isaiah 40:31: "But those who wait on the Lord shall renew their strength; they shall mount up with wings like eagles; they shall run and not be weary, they shall walk and not faint."

Glenn was an inspiration to me as a boy. He is still an inspiration to me as a man. As you read this book, I hope that he will inspire you as he has thousands of others. His was a life well lived.

Acknowledgments

No one knows better than I that there is no such thing as a self-made man. My life has been touched and influenced by many, many people along the way, and it would be impossible to name them all. Yet each one had a part in shaping my attitudes, goals, and philosophy of life, not to mention their part in my physical accomplishments.

- To the loyal friends and neighbors who did so much for my brother and me and my family at the time of the schoolhouse fire, and to the many teachers from first grade through graduate school who inspired in me a love of learning and appreciation for poetry and fine literature, encouraging me always to strive for the best in life.
- To my high school coach, Roy Varney, and my coaches at the University of Kansas, Brutus Hamilton and Bill Hargiss, who spent untold hours at my workouts teaching, correcting, drilling, and cheering me on, and the trainers, Jimmy Cox and Roland Logan, who massaged my burn-scarred legs for hours on end.
- To Jim and Margaret Heinz, who saw my drive and motivation to achieve and harnessed it along worthwhile channels by giving me work when jobs were almost nonexistent.
- To my brothers and sisters, whose love and support have continued throughout the years, and especially to my brother Floyd, who set such a wonderful example of love and courage for us all.
- To my father and mother, whose faith that I would walk again never faltered, who instilled in me the courage and determination to press on and never quit, and who wisely abstained from

treating me as an invalid but early on insisted that I pick up my responsibilities as part of the family.

- To George and Lou Sand, who encouraged me to tell this story.
- And finally, to my wife and children, who share the thanksgiving for what Christ has done in our lives and without whom our lives would be empty.

Glenn Cunningham, 1910–1988

1
The Fire

It was February 1917. The wind bit cruelly at my face as the four of us trudged across the Kansas prairie. Dirty gray light spread slowly along the flat horizon. The accumulated snow from four months of bitter winter was nearly gone, but the whine of the wind numbed us as it whipped the bottoms of our homemade cloth coats.

"Hurry up, Glenn, you're tough enough to take it," I heard Floyd, my oldest brother, holler at me through the biting air.

Four of my brothers and sisters were older and bigger than I was. I was only seven. I'd started school one year earlier, and we were again on our way to the small frame building that stood alone at a crossroads two miles from our rented farm home in Rolla, Kansas, population three hundred.

"Wish we could ride to school like other kids," Raymond muttered, walking backward against the icy blast.

"Quit complaining," Floyd told him. "They ride because they've got a lot farther to come. Anyhow, we're Cunninghams, and we can take it."

We're Cunninghams. How many times had we heard that?

"A Cunningham can stand anything," I'd heard my father say repeatedly. "Pain, hard work, tough times, and little money. We can handle anything."

Pain. I had to admit I didn't like pain—tough times and hard work I could handle, even at seven.

Floyd was thirteen, and Raymond was nine. Letha, who completed the frozen quartette that morning, was eleven. Margerie, fourteen, took care of the two youngest children at home. We'd all had to get used to tough times and hard work.

Could it have been worse?

The question didn't occur to me that day. If it had, I'm sure I couldn't have thought of any possible way life could have been more difficult. I'd learn the real truth about pain and tough times within the hour.

I hurried to catch up with Raymond. "Do I gotta help you with chores tonight, Ray?"

"You better, Glenn. Less you want another whippin' from Father."

When he wasn't farming, Father kept us fed by drilling water wells and working odd jobs. He was a dynamic and stern man, intent on ensuring that his family was cared for even in the worst of times. He insisted that we keep the family's rules; any infringement meant hard, swift discipline that usually came in the form of a buggy whip to the bottom.

The night before, I had thought I could duck out of helping milk the cows. The buggy whip had shown me otherwise. Usually, though, I'd get my work done. And I'd call it done while running. I ran everywhere: from the house to the barn, from the barn to the pasture, from home to school, from school to home. Rather than ride with my father and brothers, I'd run alongside the horses.

My father always prided himself on "just bein' practical." He'd tell me, "You've got a good pair of legs on you, Glenn. Keep usin' them, and they'll serve you well."

"Can I run in races and stuff like that?" I'd ask, hopefully. I knew I could run fast. Somewhere deep inside was the desire to see just how fast I could run in a race, like at the county fair or when I got into high school. He'd look at me hard.

"Cunninghams don't go in for fancy stuff, boy. I said you could run. That means getting your work done quicker, not showing off in front of a bunch of fool people who've got nothing better to do. Sports are a waste of time. They don't help you a bit."

We were about halfway to school when Floyd took off running. Well, it was more like a race, as Ray and I quickly followed. The three of us boys dashed across a barren Kansas wheat field.

I trailed Ray for a while and finally went by him in a sprint. He stopped running after I passed him and started walking backward to avoid the bitter wind blowing in our faces. Letha just kept walking toward the school. Pretty soon, Floyd and I approached a wooden fence that blocked our path to the school.

As Floyd approached the fence, he pushed his hands forward on the fence top and swung easily over, all in one motion. I followed a moment later, trying to jump over, but the fence was too high. I didn't make it, crashing to the ground.

Floyd started to laugh, but he saw the hurt and humiliation on my face and stopped. He opened the gate and helped me get up, brushed me off, and patted my back in congratulations.

"You have a lot of guts, Glenn Cunningham," he said. "I wouldn't have thought of trying to jump a fence that high when I was only seven."

A big grin of embarrassment and gratitude soon replaced my humiliated look.

Floyd's approval and compliment meant everything to me. He was the big brother everyone should have. He was always there for you, loyal and reliable. I'd run to and from school with Floyd when the weather permitted. I could easily make the two miles in less than fifteen minutes. Except that on this particular morning, it was too cold.

The school had a small front entrance with a shedlike covering that protected the worn double doors inside from the prairie's blowing dust in summer and drifting snows in winter.

We crowded into this little shelter, panting from the fast walk, our breath making small clouds of frost smoke when we got there. Mr. Reeves, our teacher, hadn't arrived yet. Nor had any of the nineteen other pupils he taught in the crowded single room.

"Glenn, stay outside and swing me for a while," Letha begged.

"Not me. Too cold."

Floyd and Raymond also refused. So she went alone to play in the frozen, sandy, snow-blown schoolyard.

The school had no back door, and Mr. Reeves kept the only key to the front entrance. He had told us all that if any of us arrived before he did in the morning, we'd have to use the side door, which you could open from outside. Once inside, however, you couldn't get out again until someone opened the door from the outside. We entered, and the door clicked shut behind us.

“C’mon, let’s play a game of tic-tac-toe,” Raymond suggested, and I followed him to the blackboard.

Floyd remained behind to start a fire in the big potbellied stove that was used to heat the room. The faint, dry smell of chalk powder lay on the stale air in the room.

There were thirty worn oak desks, each with a sloping top and small recessed glass inkwell. The desks were in four rows. An aisle through the center led from the door to the blackboard. Tacked along the front of the blackboard’s waist-high chalk rack were cutout replicas of rabbits and other animals, which we smaller kids had cut from stiff paper and colored with crayons.

I won a game of tic-tac-to, and then another. Raymond lost interest. He began to draw things on the blackboard.

“Look, here’s a German sub sinking Mr. Reeves’s desk,” he said, grinning at his handiwork.

“You better erase that!” I warned.

Mr. Reeves’s varnished oak desk and chair were at one end of the blackboard, which gave him a clear view of everything that went on in the room. The desk was a lighter color than ours, cleaner looking. Some of the varnish had worn off the arms of the chair. Mr. Reeves liked to tilt the chair backward when he talked to us, making the coiled spring under the chair squeak like a guinea hen.

Near the end of the day, he told us different things about the war in Europe.

“I wouldn’t be surprised if America soon joined the Allies against the Kaiser,” Mr. Reeves had said. He’d told us how more than one hundred Americans had drowned when German V-boats had torpedoed the British liner *Lusitania* off the Irish coast.

But on that cold winter morning, the war seemed remote and uninteresting. I briefly considered getting Raymond interested in another game of tic-tac-toe but instead started walking to the rear of the room, where Floyd was still working at the stove.

“Whatcha doin,’ Floyd?”

“What does it look like?” He continued to arrange the chunks of coal on top of different pieces of wood inside the stove.

“’Bout ready to start it up?”

"Yep, soon as I get some kerosene on it." I watched as he reached for the five-gallon can near the stove. Briefly, I smelled something different as he uncapped the can and began to pour. *It doesn't smell like kerosene*, I thought. *It smells more like—*

I never completed the thought as the explosion roared into my consciousness. A blinding flash seared my eyes and made my head swim. As if from hell itself, a repulsive force hurled me painfully back against the wall.

Dimly, I heard Floyd scream, "I'm on fire!"

I tried to open my eyes to see what was happening. I couldn't. Black-red, stabbing pain raced down the throbbing corridors of my mind. Suddenly I realized it.

"I'm burning, too!" The words tore from my throat. The stench of flaming cloth and flesh filled my nose. I knew somehow that it was my own.

"Get up!" Raymond was shouting in my ear. "Get up. Everything's on fire!"

He was trying to lift me from where I lay writhing on the floor. I tried to get up but couldn't. My legs buckled. They felt awful. Like they had been burned off. That frightening thought, along with the stench, sickened me. I began to vomit.

Raymond left me. I managed to get my eyes open to see him running away from me through the smoke. I tried to call after him. I couldn't. My tongue felt hot and burned, seared like my aching lungs.

I crawled painfully after Raymond. But by the time I reached the last row of desks, I knew I'd never be able to make it through the mounting flames. The heat was intense now, suffocating. I threw up again. I didn't dare look at my legs. The pain was making me cry. I tried to ease it by grabbing two desks, one on either side of the aisle, and lifting my burning legs.

Raymond, meanwhile, ran to the side door. Somewhere beyond the thick smoke and oily, licking flames, I could hear him pounding it, yelling for Letha to open it from the outside. I wasn't aware of Floyd, also ahead of me, crawling, clawing his way as he worked toward the side door.

Letha had heard the explosion. She had turned in her swing seat to stare at the terrible red flames that suddenly brightened the schoolhouse windows. She raced to the side door and jerked it open.

"Throw sand on us," Floyd screamed at Letha as she and Raymond led us outside. I followed my older brother's example as he hurled himself to the ground and repeatedly rolled, trying to smother the flames.

It did no good. Nor could Letha and Raymond claw away much of the frozen sand.

Floyd staggered to his feet, still on fire in several places. "Home," he sobbed. "We gotta get *home*!" He began to run.

Raymond and Letha had been busily slapping at my body, trying to beat out the flames licking at my waist. Now we all stared in horror.

"Floyd—stop!" Letha screeched. She leaped to her feet and ran after him. Raymond helped me as I followed, hobbling. Floyd was running nearly naked. Only the top of his burned jacket remained. There was just a baked and blackened body between that and his smoking shoes. His eyes were wide and wild as we caught up with him.

Letha removed her coat and helped him struggle into it. The effort tore loose several lumpy pieces of flesh.

Floyd saw but said nothing. Instead, he started running again.

As we followed, I glanced at my legs for the first time. Both pant legs had burned away, and the sight of the deep burns on my legs made me vomit again.

I hadn't run a hundred feet before I became dizzy. I fell headlong to the hard ground. Raymond saw and ran back to help.

"You gotta keep going," he murmured in my ear. "Get up."

Keep going for two miles? Impossible.

"When we get home, Mother will know what to do," my brother yelled, shaking me by the shoulders. "C'mon, Glenn," Raymond pleaded. "You can't just lie there."

No, of course not. Father would expect more than that. Never quit. Run on. Work your problem out by yourself whenever you can. That's what Henry "Clint" Cunningham always told his kids.

I stumbled to my feet and began my hobbling run again. Strangely, I no longer felt the searing leg pains. I wondered why. I wondered if Floyd's pain had melted away, too.

A hundred yards more, and Floyd fell. Letha had him up again almost at once.

"You're gonna make it home," she told him fiercely. "I *know* you're gonna make it, Floyd."

Floyd stared vacantly at his sister's tear-filled eyes. Then he nodded and got up.

We were underway again, slower now. Then I remembered something that all of us had forgotten in the excitement. Mother would *not* be home. Neither would Father.

Mom had spent the night at Uncle John's house to care for my grandmother Nancy Kent Cunningham. Dad had gone for her that morning after we kids had left for school. Uncle John lived three miles from us. Father had announced that he would be going there to get her that morning.

Only Margerie and the two small children were at home. *Margerie is only fourteen*, I told myself. *She won't know how to treat burns this bad!* I felt like giving up again. A sense of self-preservation kept propelling me, head down, eyes barely open to keep the burning sensation at a minimum, toward that squat, square farmhouse that held the only relief available.

"Almost there, Glenn, almost there," Raymond kept urging me.

Letha was nearly dragging Floyd the last few steps to the door. "Margerie!" Letha yelled. "Margerie, open the door."

The front door of the two-story farmhouse swung back, and Margerie gasped at the horror. "Oh no!" Her hand flew to her mouth, stifling a scream as Floyd collapsed inside the door with a loud groan. Margerie caught him in her arms.

"Quick! Help me get them over to the bed," Margerie ordered Letha and Raymond as she grasped Floyd under his arms.

Our parents slept in a double bed in the downstairs part of the house, also a combined kitchen and living room. My sisters and brother lifted Floyd and me into their bed. Then Margerie gave more orders.

"Raymond, go get Mother and Father. Letha, get Mr. Heinrich." Mr. Heinrich lived in a farmhouse closer to ours than Uncle John's, where our parents were.

Margerie was crying silently as she gingerly removed my burned clothing. I was screeching again from the pain, and my sister bent down quickly to kiss me before turning her attention to Floyd.

Floyd was staring glassy-eyed at the ceiling, not making a sound. Margerie removed his still smoking shoes and placed them outside the back door on top of a homemade sled built to haul water from Mr. Heinrich's windmill-operated well. We had no well of our own.

Mr. Heinrich, an old German who lived alone, soon came hurrying in with Letha close behind. He carried a dirty bottle of linseed oil from his workshop.

"Ach! Get bandages," Mr. Heinrich ordered as he stared pityingly at my brother and me. "We need many bandages. Margerie, maybe you have some old bed sheets, ja?"

As my sister helped, the clucking older man clumsily wrapped my throbbing wounds. The pain proved too much, and I fainted.

The next voice I heard was soft and soothing, close to my face. It was my mother.

"The doctor is on his way from Rolla," she said, the other family members cooling my feverish forehead with a wet washcloth. I opened my eyes. Mother was trying hard not to cry. She and Father made a point of not showing emotion. But her wide-set gray eyes were shiny and moist. Father was staring hard down at Floyd. His glance, usually bright blue, now looked dull with hurt.

The other children stood crowded at the foot of the bed, silent, watching fearfully. Mother turned to them.

"Raymond, you fetch me some water to heat. The doctor will need it."

Father saw me gritting my teeth against the pain, trying not to faint again. He moved closer and put a hand on my upper arm, giving it a little squeeze. He said nothing. Raymond burst in, carrying a pail of water. "The sled," he said. "It's gone!"

"What do you mean, gone?" Father demanded.

"It's all burnt up. Nothin' but ashes left. Floyd's shoes musta set it on fire."

I was screaming again from the agony. Mother was holding me

down as best she could when Dr. Hansen arrived. The doctor merely glanced at me and then gave his attention to Floyd.

He was a young doctor, just starting his practice. I turned my head to watch as Dr. Hansen placed a stethoscope against my brother's chest. The doctor looked solemn as he moved the disc from one place to another, listening to the weakened sounds coming from Floyd's blackened body.

When my turn came, the doctor had Mother bring the hot water. "Put these in it and let them dissolve," he ordered, handing her some big pink disinfectant pills. While Mother held me, Dr. Hansen used the solution to swab my deep burns.

"That stings awful," I screeched.

"Shush," Mother commanded gently. "Floyd didn't make nearly so much noise."

When she finished, the young doctor patted me. "You can stop crying now, son," he said quietly. Dr. Hansen stood up and motioned for Father to follow him outside. As the door closed upon them, Mother and I could hear Father saying firmly, "Doctor, we want the truth."

Dr. Hansen's words were barely audible: "With Glenn, the big danger is infection. If it comes, both legs would have to be amputated. Regardless, I doubt if he'll be able to walk again."

The doctor was silent for a minute. "With Floyd, there's not much we can do."

We learned later that a community club of farm women had met at the schoolhouse the night before and rebuilt the fire we'd had during the day. It hadn't died out by the time the four of us arrived that fateful morning.

The club members had brought gasoline with them. The gas had carelessly been left in the kerosene can with no identification to warn us of what could happen.

And the worst had happened.

2

Till We Meet Again

The first-floor room was about twenty feet square on each side and had three windows. A wood-burning heating stove with a shiny brown enamel finish stood in the center. Once, I had enjoyed watching the dancing flames through the stove's small isinglass door windows. Now the cherry-red color looked ugly. It brought back terrifying memories of the school fire.

Against the opposite wall, beneath one of the windows, were a homemade wooden table and several straight-backed chairs, some of them quite wobbly. At one corner, my place was where the red-and-white checkered oilcloth barely held together. I hadn't sat there for nearly a week now. A second and larger stove for cooking stood against a third wall beside an unpainted corner cupboard.

Mother was standing before this cupboard, peeling potatoes for dinner. From the back, she looked hardly bigger than Margerie. She had pulled her fading brown hair into a loose, wispy bun. A long gray skirt almost hid her worn, small black shoes.

"Mom?"

"Yes?"

"Floyd was humming 'Till We Meet Again' last night."

"I know."

"You heard him, too?"

"No. But Father told me."

Father had sat up with me.

"He can't help it," Father had whispered, trying to get me interested in the new Sears catalog that had recently arrived. "Floyd doesn't even know we're in the room with him."

Floyd and I each lay in our beds now, making the downstairs part of our two-room home pretty crowded with the double bed there, too.

Father had carried the smaller beds down from the second-floor room where we normally slept.

Day after day, Floyd lay in his bed without speaking, white-faced and seldom moving. He ate very little. If he needed attention, he opened his eyes and stared vacantly at us until someone came to him.

But what happened at night—usually after midnight—bothered me even more. My older brother would suddenly start to hum softly. He hummed the same hymn over and over: "God Be with You Till We Meet Again."

I knew Floyd liked that tune. He'd learned it at the revival meetings that were held now and then at the schoolhouse whenever a circuit-riding evangelist came through our remote part of the state. Often, several families would get together at home for Bible study and prayer. It had been at one of those home meetings that I'd felt I should become a Christian.

My prayer that night had been simple: "God, I'm sorry I'm a sinner. Please make me all right inside." It would be years before I knew just how seriously God had taken that small act of commitment.

Now, though, the shock of a double tragedy was telling on all the members of my family. They were all worn out. The neighbors, Jeff Cox, Grandma Ward, Les Garmon, and George Erhart, knew that my grieving parents welcomed any opportunity to sleep upstairs with their other children and often came to sit with Floyd and me at night. For my parents, it meant they'd have to sleep on the floor. But it also meant a welcome escape from the moans and the constant foul odors from our oozing wounds. My legs remained an ugly, awful-looking red.

They pained me more at night for some reason.

Nearly every night, I had terrible dreams about the fire. I dreamed that my legs had burned away, leaving only nubs. I would never walk again. I could only hobble after the other kids.

One night while having this same nightmare, I screamed so loudly that I awakened everyone. Letha had been dozing in the big chair while trying to do her homework and became annoyed. "Oh, shut up, Glenn," she cried, shaking me peevishly. "Shut *up*!"

After Letha had gone to bed, Mother fussed over me, helping me calm down. "It's not right," I told her, "the way you all have to wait on us."

"That's what a family is for," she said, fluffing my pillow and tucking the blankets back in. "Now, you go to sleep." But I couldn't. The pain in my legs was tearing at my insides.

"If only I could move them," I sobbed to Mother, "even just a little." She sat on the edge of my bed and took me in her arms. "It takes time, honey," she soothed.

"Mom?"

"Yes?"

"My legs smell awful. Could the flesh be rotting?"

"Shush!"

"Does that mean the infection has set in? Like Dr. Hansen said it might?"

I felt her arms tighten around me. "You just quit that kind of talk," she said firmly. Then she released me and stood up. "C'mon, I'll get the checkerboard, but just one game, mind you. No more."

My legs had been drawing up a bit more each day. I could no longer bend either one at the knee. The young doctor hadn't placed my legs in traction.

The ninth morning after the fire, I awoke and immediately glanced at Floyd. He lay still, eyes closed.

After breakfast, Father came and stood looking down at Floyd before leaving for work. He stood silently for several minutes while we all watched the love wash over his drawn face.

"Floyd?" Father asked softly. "It's breakfast time, boy."

My brother's sunken eyes opened slowly. They seemed to glow as he stared at Father. Father must have seen something in that glance that encouraged him.

"Mother, this boy is hungry!" he said loudly for our benefit. "Warm him up some of that chicken soup you made." Floyd permitted Margerie to spoon-feed him the broth from a small bowl. It was the first time I had seen him accept soup. Father was grinning as he left for work.

The doctor came later that morning. He nodded but made no

comment when Mother told him about the soup. Floyd was lying motionless again with his eyes closed.

Evening arrived. I watched my brothers and sisters steal sober glances at Floyd as they sat thoughtfully at the dinner table. When it came time to retire, Mother announced that she would sit up with Floyd and me.

Mother and I spoke in whispers for a while. Then I pretended to sleep for her sake. More wispy hair than usual had worked loose from her bun. She looked tired. I felt restless. There was a full moon outside, and it made the room bright. Father had placed Floyd's bed foot-to-foot against mine, and I could see him. He appeared to be asleep.

I must have dozed, for I awoke with a start. I sensed that something was wrong.

I looked at Floyd. His dim eyes were open wide. He was staring right at me. My older brother's mouth began to quiver. He started to hum the hymn again softly. I could barely recognize the low sound, yet Mother awoke at once. She stood up quickly and bent over Floyd.

"We . . ." I heard my brother gasp. "We . . ."

"Yes, honey, what is it?" Mother whispered.

"We . . . till we . . ." Floyd raised himself slightly as he strained to go on.

"Till we meet at Jesus's feet," Mother finished, singing gently for him.

Floyd's nod was barely perceptible. "Meet . . . meet . . . at Je . . . at Jesus's feet," he managed to moan.

He said no more. Instead, he took Mother's hand and pressed it weakly to his lips. Floyd's pale face looked ethereal, as if he saw angels in the moonlight.

Tears slid down Mother's face. I had never seen her cry before.

Floyd died that night. I had lost my hero and best friend.

The undertaker, a skinny older man who raised pigs, came the next day. He spoke little as he made the arrangements. After he left, Father took apart the other bed. His face looked gray as ashes as he carried the cot back upstairs.

Floyd's funeral service was in the yard of our home. It was an overcast day, windy, raw, and cold. A couple of dozen relatives and friends stood bareheaded outside, listening. My parents remained indoors. They sat stiffly in chairs by an open window of the first floor, where I lay. In her lap, Mother clutched a small black book. I had seen her Bible only once before. She had shown me where she kept it in a trunk in our attic.

The rest of us remained inside, too. We listened tearfully to the solemn words of an older adult whom Father had brought from somewhere.

Margerie sat white-faced on the floor, holding in her lap the two weeping youngest members of our family, little Johnny and Melva. Raymond slumped at the dining table, his head on his arms. Letha stayed beside my bed, sobbing and gripping my hand hard.

When the brief funeral service ended, several men lifted Floyd's new pine coffin onto a horse-drawn lumber wagon. Neighbors and friends buried my brother at a nearby cemetery. None of our family went.

I lay in bed, wondering if Floyd was with Jesus. What did that mean? The people at those Bible studies had said that was what happened when a Christian died. I didn't understand it, but I fervently hoped Floyd was happy now and without pain.

After the funeral, Dr. Hansen told us he was leaving the area for a while to be near his recently widowed mother.

"Am I gonna get well?" I asked impulsively. He didn't say anything more to me.

"I've arranged for another doctor to take care of him," he told my parents. Then he was gone.

I came to hate the new doctor. I gritted my teeth each time I heard this impatient older man drive into the yard in his Model T.

"Why can't he take time to soak the bandages first, as Dr. Hansen did?" I complained to Mother. "He rips them off, scabs and all!"

Mother had no answer. My legs had grown steadily worse. They were so bad now that I could hardly stand the pain from just resting them on the bed. I'd find myself fantasizing about walking again, running again, and just standing again.

I tried to recall what it was like to place one foot in front of the other without thinking about it.

I'd remember incidents like trotting several miles beside a team of horses pulling a wagon back from the field. The summer before, I'd done this often when Floyd, Ray, and I were out with Father gleaning the stubble fields to get fodder for the stock. Everyone else would climb on board to ride back home when the wagon was ready. Sometimes five miles or more, I'd run alongside until we reached the barn. Would I ever be able to do that again?

One day Raymond discovered that the pain could be relieved a little if I lifted my legs clear of the bed. Mother was pleased with the small discovery.

"The rest of you children help do this whenever you can," she told them. "Take turns."

The others grumbled, but they did help. Someone would stand at the foot of the bed, holding my heels to keep the aching legs elevated. I hadn't the strength to raise my legs by myself.

To add to my misery, a huge boil, the size of a baseball, formed on my left hip. Until now, I had been able to get some relief from my bedsores by rolling onto my left side. I still had a large burn on my right leg, preventing me from lying on that side. Now I had to remain on my back constantly.

I overheard Father ask the new doctor, Dr. Tucker, about the boil. "Does that mean the infection has gotten inside the boy's body?"

"That's exactly what it means."

"What can we do about it?"

"I don't know of anything you can do about it. Just pray, I reckon."

After Dr. Tucker left, I told Father what I'd heard.

"Does that mean they're gonna cut my leg off?" I asked fearfully.

"Naw!"

"Dr. Hansen said that's what would happen if the infection came."

"Doctors ain't always right."

That throbbing boil seemed to give the older doctor a new excuse to hurt me. Sometimes it was all Mother could do to hold me down while this rough man lanced the boil and drained it.

One afternoon Father happened to be home early and helped Dr. Tucker as I lay screaming from the pain.

"Hold the boy still while I get something from my bag," Dr. Tucker snapped at him. When the doctor returned, he was angry.

"Someone has taken my bag," he announced. "It must have been one of your kids."

Johnny and Melva had done it. Hearing my cries, they had slipped into the room, grabbed the doctor's black bag, and ran out into the yard to hide it. Father paddled them both but did it lightly, hardly able to conceal a sad smile.

"The children did it only in love," Mother tried to assure the indignant doctor. "They must have thought it was the bag that was making Glenn yell so."

Our parents had taught us to love one another. They had taught us to love strangers, too. The family of Clint Cunningham never turned away a hungry person, poor though we were.

Our neighbors continued to show concern. Some brought food and small gifts. Others took turns helping Mother with the housework. One afternoon a stout lady from Elkhart visited Mother. I heard her telling Mother that the schoolhouse, which had burned to the ground that terrible morning, would not be rebuilt before fall.

The visitor had a loud voice. When she prepared to leave, I could still hear her talking outside.

"You may as well face it, my dear," she told Mother. "Glenn's going to be a cripple the rest of his life."

When Mother returned, the look on my face told her I'd heard. She came over to the bed and sat down carefully on the edge of the mattress. I hurled the words at her: "I'm not going to be a cripple. She's wrong, you know! Wrong, you hear?"

Mother reached out and brushed my hair back from my sweaty forehead. She leaned over and kissed me on the cheek. "Yes, Glenn, I know she's wrong."

The words came soothingly, gently.

"I will walk again?"

"Yes, Glenn, you'll walk again."

"I will!" And now I was screaming. "I will! I will!"

3
You Mean Now?

Three months had passed since the fire. Dr. Hansen had returned, and for that, I was glad. But my legs weren't healing.

"Why can't you make them better?" I asked him through clenched teeth as Mother helped to remove the blood-caked bandages gently. Dr. Hansen paused to pat me on the head. "It takes time, Glenn," he said soberly.

"You *always* say that," I shouted, suddenly hating him. "I know what you're thinking. I can see it in your face every time you come here. You're thinking I'm never gonna get well; my legs are always gonna be like this!"

Mother tried to silence me, but the angry words gushed from me in a torrent. Did they have any idea how it felt to lie here day after day? How *could* they know? They didn't have the endless pain. Every waking hour, it was there. Every minute. Every second.

My outburst to Mother, vowing to walk again, took hold in my mind, slowly at first, then with more and more determination as I fought to find something, anything, to keep my mind off the horrible pain. I would visualize myself running in competition, seeing myself with chest thrust out, arms rhythmically churning in time with my feet, and putting more distance between myself and others in a race.

Oh, God, how I want to run again.

Instead, I'd be rudely pulled back to reality by the awful ache in my legs, the throbbing boil, and now the stabbing bedsores that continued to spread over my body. Finally, a flood of tears came, choking off the wild thoughts and angry words. As Mother took me in her arms, I collapsed back on the bed, sobbing and exhausted.

"Continue to use the salve," Dr. Hansen told her as he finished and stood up.

Mother searched his face with her glance. "That's all?"

He shrugged. "That's all I know to do."

The salve smelled sickeningly sweet. I grew to loathe it. But Mother used it every day.

"Glenn, we just got to," she would say, patiently kneading the limp muscles and carefully avoiding the running sores.

To help pass the time, Mother played word games with me while working in the kitchen, like guessing how high I would be able to count before a fresh kettle of water would begin to boil on the stove. I made up other games. A wainscoted ceiling over my head was made of three-inch-wide boards painted gray. As I lay in bed, I studied these repeatedly, just as I had every other thing in that crowded room. I could close my eyes and picture it all. "How many boards would you guess don't go across?" I would challenge Mother. Or maybe "How far in is the one with the two knots?" Nearly always, Mother would guess wrong. I suspect she did it on purpose.

I used another trick to get through the dragging hours when I was alone. I tried to remember all the happy times before the fire.

I remembered running to school with Floyd and how he challenged me to be faster and stronger.

I thought of my little yellow terrier, Jack. That dog could do nearly anything. He would sit up, bark, roll over, and play dead. I remembered when I used to lift Jack into the lower branches of a tree if we saw a squirrel overhead, and that silly dog would immediately try to catch the critter by climbing up from one limb to the next.

I liked most to recall the trip I had made across Kansas in a big covered wagon with a white canvas top. I was five when my father, whooping and hollering like a drunken cowboy, drove up in a cloud of dust with the wagon and four panting horses.

"Hoo-rah!" he yelled. "Everybody out to help me get ready."

"Ready for what?" Mother called, holding her long skirt above her ankles as we all ran out to meet him.

"We're a-headin' west. Just like the early settlers."

"Well, I never . . ." Mother gasped as we kids screeched with pleasure. Although she had known about the trip beforehand, Mother liked the unexpected, fun-loving way my father sometimes behaved, even when it included the impulsive decision to move to a new area simply because he had become restless.

Mother had never been a match for his strong self-sufficiency, so she had adopted an attitude of willingness to accept the unexpected, a philosophy that reflected her love for the man.

School was out, and the weather was pleasant. It was a good time to travel, Father pointed out. He promptly loaded all our possessions into the wagon. Everything that would fit, that is. The rest he cheerfully gave away to friends.

"My pots and pans," Mother wailed when Father left no space for them. "I can't leave my pots and pans."

"No need to," Father assured her with a wide grin. He hung the pots under the wagon, and there they swung back and forth between the big wheels as we jogged slowly westward over the rolling prairie.

"Father, where are we going?" Margerie asked as we left.

Father scratched behind one ear, trying to look serious. "Danged if I know, honey," he answered. "Does it matter?"

We wandered westward through Kansas, following the wheat harvest. Whenever we found a farmer in need of help, my mother and my two older sisters would work beside us in the hot fields, often twelve hours a day. When one man's crop was in, we would move on to help another. Sometimes Mother would be paid extra for cooking for our employer's hungry workers.

After about 250 miles of such wagon living, Father decided we should move indoors for a while and rented the farm at Rolla. It was there that Floyd died from the burns he received in the fire.

It appeared that I would never travel again. Dr. Hansen was concerned because I was becoming increasingly bitter.

"Maybe a change would help," he suggested. "Let's move him upstairs."

Now I had a new world to discover. I had lived in this world before, but I hadn't seen it.

"You see that place at the top of the wallpaper where the ceiling begins?" I asked Mother as she sat on the bed, massaging my useless legs. "You look at it long enough, and it starts talkin' to you. It starts askin' questions."

There was an endless design in the wallpaper, about five inches high, at the top of each wall. It appeared to spell R-U-R-U-R-U, over and over. As I lay in bed watching it, the unusual design seemed to ask again and again, "Are you ready, Glenn Cunningham, to be an invalid for the rest of your life? Are you? Are you? Are you?"

Another Kansas summer had arrived. Now the air in the upper room where I lay became still, stiflingly hot. One sweltering August afternoon, I heard Dr. Hansen climbing the stairs with Mother. After taking my temperature and trying unsuccessfully, as usual, to bend my stiff legs, he looked at me thoughtfully.

"Glenn, for six months, you've been telling us that you are going to walk again," he said. "Do you still believe that?"

"Yes, sir."

"All right, let's try it."

"You mean *now*?"

He smiled slightly. "Now."

They both watched as I pushed myself slowly upright in the bed. Bracing myself in position with one hand, I used the other to move my right leg an inch toward the edge of the bed. Then another inch, then the left leg the same way. Sweat broke out on my body. Mother was staring.

I got my legs over the edge. They slanted downward, not touching the floor. Mother and Dr. Hansen took up positions on either side to help if necessary. I brushed them aside. "Lemme be!"

My head was reeling as I pushed myself the rest of the way upward and outward so my feet touched the floor. I tried to take a step. I couldn't. My legs wouldn't move. I would have fallen, but Mother and the doctor caught me. I cried bitterly as they lifted me gently onto my rumpled bed.

Dr. Hansen stared at me thoughtfully. He patted my shoulder, then led the way downstairs, where I heard him and Mother speak in low tones.

They weren't going to amputate my legs, but I could tell the doctor didn't think I would ever use them much. I was glad when Father got home that evening, and I heard his booted feet on the stairs. He always came to see me before getting cleaned up for supper.

"Father, I need something," I told him.

"What's that, boy?"

"Our big chair downstairs. I need it right here. Right beside my bed."

His light blue eyes became thoughtful.

"That's our best chair, son."

"I know it."

He looked tired. He drilled wells for a living, and it was a tough job. We could hear my brothers and sisters playing tag in the yard below.

"I need your chair, Father," I said as he walked to a window and looked down into the yard. I knew he liked to sit in it after a long day drilling. But I had to ask. Father turned and studied my face. Then he nodded.

"Sure," he said. "Sure. I'll bring 'er up to you, Glenn."

That sturdy, homemade chair became my exercise machine. I could pull myself slowly from the bed to land weakly in the chair seat by grasping its arms.

Then, using one arm of the chair as a crutch to pull me erect, I would lean against the back as I inched my way painfully around to the front. There, I would collapse again. The exercises also made it possible for me to use the chamber pot without always calling for help.

Occasionally someone would use the chair and forget to return it to its place beside my bed. When that happened, Father would scold whoever was guilty. Without the chair close by, I would be obliged to slide from the bed to the floor and then use my elbows to squirm, dragging my useless legs behind me, until I reached the chair. The sores had gradually healed, but my legs continued to pain me almost all the time. Everyone sympathized with me, even the neighbor kids who came to visit. But I could tell that no one felt it was doing much good.

"Aw, you ain't never gonna walk again," one boy told me.

"Yes, he is," Mother told him quickly. "You bet he is."

4
Christmas 1917

My exercises continued for weeks. The day before Christmas, 1917, my mother was sitting at the foot of the bed, rubbing my legs as usual, with a white smudge of flour on one cheek. She had been baking bread and Christmas cookies all morning.

"I have a present for you," I told her.

"Where would you get a present?" she teased.

I paid no attention. "To get it, you gotta go and stand by the door."

Smiling, Mother did as I asked.

"Close your eyes."

When she did, I slipped from the bed. I took a faltering step toward her. Then another.

"Now open them—quick, Mother!"

My head was starting to swim. Mother's small gray eyes widened. Then she made a choking sound as she rushed forward to catch me in her arms. We sank to the floor together, hugging one another. I saw my mother cry for the second and last time in my life. I was bawling, too.

That afternoon, when school let out for the holidays, Mother had me demonstrate my new ability to my brothers and sisters. Margerie and Letha both cried as they threw their arms happily around me. Raymond's eyes were shining.

It was nearly dark before Father came home from drilling wells. From his quick steps on the stairs, I could tell that someone had told him. His face was still grimy with sweat and dust as he strode into the room.

"So!" he said, grinning as he stood looking down at me. "So!" He didn't have to say more as our glances met and held.

I was awakened before daylight the next morning as my brothers and sisters scrambled from the bed. They hurried downstairs to see what Santa Claus had left for them. I couldn't follow.

"Whoa," I heard Father's voice suddenly roar from below. "Everybody just whoa right where you are."

Father quickly climbed the stairs. He bent over my bed in the dark and said gently, "We go down to Christmas together, boy. You and me."

Father lifted me bodily. His muscular arms felt hard as tree limbs as he hoisted me easily onto his shoulder.

"You watch your head now," he cautioned as he ducked so we could reach the landing at the top of the stairs. Father stopped.

"Look what I have here," he announced loudly.

Below, the noisy room suddenly became quiet. Every face turned upward, eyes staring in the soft candlelight from the Christmas tree made of tumbleweed.

Father stood still, giving me a chance to see what I hadn't seen in months: my parents' double bed, which Mother had already made up; the folded-down dining table with its red-checkered oilcloth under the window on the opposite wall.

"Santa just couldn't seem to find us a regular tree this year," Father continued in a loud voice as we started down. "But he sure gave us a big present to put under it."

"Merry Christmas, Glenn," Mother called in a choked voice. The others echoed the greeting as they crowded together. Letha and Margerie kissed me, and I could feel their cheeks wet with tears.

"I wish Floyd could be here to see you," Margerie whispered quickly in my ear. Then everyone was talking at once.

"I'm walking again," I yelled to no one in particular as Father lowered me carefully into Mother's lap. "I'm walking again. I told you I would walk again."

"It's a miracle, Glenn," Mother said softly. "It has to be a miracle." Her face was shining.

"It's no miracle," Father contradicted her proudly. "It just took plain ol' Cunningham guts." He winked broadly at me and added, "Right, Glenn?"

Then we set about opening our presents.

There were only a few. The scattered gifts lay on the floor, decorated with bright dabs of scarlet and green, unusually small packages that made a little pile beneath the withered gray tumbleweed that served as a tree. A dozen small candles burned in little holders, clipped fast in various places to limbs of the three-foot-high weed. We had no electricity.

Tumbleweed is a densely branched plant that grows on the prairie, usually several feet high. These weeds break away easily from their roots and are rolled about endlessly by the wind when they die. No one wants the tangled things, except maybe to burn.

However, no evergreen trees grew in our area. They had to be shipped in for Christmas.

"And there's no money for that," Father explained.

So he and the kids had gone out and found this especially large tumbleweed rolling about behind Mr. Heinrich's chicken farm. Ray had mounted the weed atop a small wooden box to make it look taller. The girls had draped an old sheet around the chest to hide its ugliness. And they had decorated this Christmas tree with pictures cut from a mail-order catalog.

Dr. Hansen was pleased when he saw that I could take a few faltering steps. But he was cautious.

"Maybe by spring, Glenn," he answered when I asked if I could go outdoors. "Your knees are loosening up. But that right leg is still pretty weak."

It seemed forever before the weather warmed and it was OK to go outside. By then, much of the pain had finally gone, leaving an incredible stiffness in both legs. How good the sun felt against my neck. How clean the spring air smelled! It had been a year and two months since the schoolhouse fire.

"Even the cows have wondered where you were," Father said, a twinkle in his eye. "Now you can help us with the chores again, Glenn."

I could begin by cleaning the dirt from the plowshares when he came in from the fields that afternoon.

And then, an odd series of events began. I'd spent months in bed, writhing in pain and trying desperately to cling to a desire to walk and run again; now, when I could at least get outside, being expected to pitch in was not to my liking.

"It's too soon to expect me to work," I complained to Mother after Father had gone. My leg and foot constantly hurt, causing me to hobble.

One day after school, when he and Raymond had fed the stock, Father found me sitting on the kitchen floor complaining to Mother about the leg.

"C'mon, boy, we're all gonna chase rabbits on the prairie," he invited cheerfully.

I shook my head. "I couldn't even catch a turtle."

"Well, you could help some, I reckon. Mother says we need the meat."

"No."

As we talked, I had been stretching out my right leg as far as it would go, exercising the muscles and tendons. Now his face grew stern as he reached down and lifted me bodily from the floor.

"I said you're going *with* us, boy!" His eyes were suddenly blue frost.

"Yes, sir," I said quickly, and he set me down with a little warning shake.

Father was awfully strong for a small man. When he drilled wells, he used an eight-hundred-pound steel bit. Several times we kids had seen him maneuver that great bit from a wagon by himself, straining so fiercely in his determination to do it that the veins stood out on his temples.

Mother moved to my side.

"I better come along," she told him, sliding a steadying arm about my waist as I stood up.

Father's eyes were still hard as he stared at her. "What about dinner, then?" he asked her sharply.

"I must wait, remember?" she said carefully. "Until we catch the rabbits." There was quiet defiance in her as she returned his glance. Father snorted. He went outside without another word.

The others were waiting. Father had the wagon ready for me. He lifted me onto the seat, not speaking, and then helped Mother up.

He handed her the reins for the two horses and turned away, again without a word.

The wagon creaked as we followed the others out onto the flat prairie. Prairie cottontails are swift and hard to catch. You have to run them down and corner them before they can dive into a hole.

While Mother and I watched from the wagon seat, Letha caught one of the furry little brown-and-white creatures by its hind legs just as it was disappearing into its den. Father shouted his approval, and Raymond dispatched the rabbit with a heavy stick to its head. Then Father and Margerie cornered another in a small brush-grown gully.

"Everybody help!" Father called to us excitedly. "Mother, Glenn, c'mon! Help us surround him."

Mother climbed down quickly from the wagon seat. She turned around and reached up for me.

"I just can't do it," I whispered, holding back.

"C'mon, Glenn," Father called impatiently. Mother looked up at me pleadingly. "Do as he says," she muttered. "Dr. Hansen said you must exercise."

"I can't." I knew that the more I exercised the legs, the stiffer they became until the stiffness combined with a return of the pain, leaving me in agony. Father was running toward us.

"I said come on, boy!" he shouted.

I began to cry as he reached up and lifted me from the seat with a single sweeping movement.

"Now, walk!" he barked, setting me down and pushing me gently toward my watching brothers and sisters.

I took a step and nearly fell.

"Go on," he ordered sternly.

I hobbled forward. *Can't Father understand that I'm still not well?* I thought bitterly.

The rabbit, meanwhile, had escaped.

"We'll find us another," Father snapped. "Let's try that draw over yonder."

He motioned us all forward. He stood still, watching me hobble past him, following slowly after Mother and the others.

The site that Father had indicated was a couple of hundred yards away. I was stumbling unhappily along, already well behind the others, when I heard his footsteps approaching behind me. I listened to the plodding steps of a horse, too.

"You're moving awful slow, boy," Father barked. "Here."

He had gone back to the wagon and unhitched one of the horses. Now he thrust the animal's gritty black tail into my hands. "Hang on to that," he ordered. "Let's go."

I hung on reluctantly as Father led the horse forward. I could see the others grinning as the walking horse pulled me along after it—all except Mother.

We captured three more of the darting little rabbits before darkness stopped the hunting.

"All right, that's enough for dinner, I reckon," Father announced. "Let's head back for the wagon."

I could feel him watching me again as Letha helped me get the horse pointed in that direction. It was a quarter mile to the wagon, and my legs were hurting now. I had to grit my teeth to keep from complaining as the horse surged forward, nearly pulling me off balance. I had taken but a dozen floundering steps when Father suddenly called, *"Whoa!"*

I turned and looked back fearfully. Father was making straight for me, but his strong face wore a pleased expression.

"Time to change horses, boy!" he announced, smiling as he hoisted me atop his thick shoulders. "Don't you go spurrin' me none, though. I'm tired."

And that was how we returned to the wagon: he steadied me upright with both his hands about my waist. The others were smiling again. But this time, I was happy as I clung to Father, my face buried in his clean black hair. The proud way he held me gave me a warm feeling inside.

The gentle warmth of spring blended into the heat of summer. Now the planting was replaced with new farm chores. With food always short, my family regularly sought fresh meat by chasing down rabbits on the prairie. Father always made sure that I went along to help, but I might as well have stayed home. I could muster only a little, useless, hippity-hop gait. He didn't act pleased.

"You *run,* boy!" he advised me late one afternoon as we set out in the wagon with several of the others. "Don't complain. Just try. Keep tryin'. You'll never catch a rabbit if you don't try."

That night, as Mother tucked me into bed and massaged my aching legs, tears slid down my cheeks as I tried to explain my feelings.

"How can I run?' I asked her bitterly. "The fire destroyed my foot arch, making my right leg much shorter than the other."

"You do the best you can, Glenn," she soothed, kissing me.

I had found it difficult, to say the least, to put my fantasies into action. I'd lain in bed for months, dreaming about walking and running; now that I was up and around, it was a different matter altogether. I still kept my dreams, but it was turning out to be very tough to put them into action. I wanted to run again—really run—but I needed something to help me get to the point where I'd be strong enough to do it.

That summer, I got an idea. I went to Father when he brought our team of horses home from a day in the fields.

"You remember that day when you had me hang on to the tail of one of the horses?" I asked.

He nodded, using a sleeve to wipe sweat from his face.

"Mebbe you'd let me hang on to some of the cows like that?" I asked hopefully. When he frowned, I added quickly, "It sure would be good for my legs. I can't use the horses now. You always need 'em in the fields."

"I wouldn't want you upsettin' them milk cows, boy," he warned, still frowning.

"Oh, no, sir. I'd sure be right careful."

"All right. But you make sure, or you'll be sorry."

After that, at least once a day, I would grab the tail of one of the cows and let the surprised animal pull me slowly. By fall, my legs were much stronger.

They had rebuilt the burned-down school. It was a big day for me when I enrolled at the new one-room building on opening day that fall. Often throughout that day, I saw Floyd's fire-blackened face before me.

“Those kids at school have nicknamed me ‘Scarlegs,’” I told Father angrily that evening. “They’re sayin’ I’ll never be able to run again!”

“Never mind them. They’re just jealous ’cause you’re showin’ enough guts to try and lick this thing.”

That was his philosophy: never quit. Always get out there and try to overcome, no matter what.

5
The Snowstorm

I was nine when the terrible flu epidemic struck the entire world in the fall of 1918. Before it ended, twenty million people would die, more than 500,000 of whom were Americans.

"Nearly everybody in Rolla has it," Father told us grimly when he returned from the village one afternoon. "Dr. Hansen is going crazy making calls."

The undertaker remained busy, too. The skinny older man had warned Father about the high fever.

"It usually doesn't last more than a day," the undertaker said. "If you find yourself gettin' delirious from it, look out. That's probably the end."

"People are scared," I overheard Father tell Mother. "Those who don't have the flu won't come out to help the others. I told Dr. Hansen I'd help." Instead, Father landed in bed with influenza. So did everyone else in our family but me. Ben Garmon, an eighteen-year-old neighbor who lived to the east of us, also escaped.

"Why do you reckon you're not gettin' it?" I asked Ben.

"I had it already," he explained. "Back home. I been wonderin' why you ain't caught it."

"I 'spect mebbe God just ain't lettin' me catch it," I guessed. "I reckon He knows I'm needed to help the others now."

"You believe that?"

"Floyd always said that God works like that. He takes care of you if you live well."

Ben looked at me pityingly. "How come God let Floyd die, then?" he scoffed. "That's like sayin' Floyd wasn't good."

I couldn't answer that, and it bothered me.

"C'mon, we got work to do," I reminded him.

The work hurt my right leg, for we were putting in long days. Ben and I worked from daylight until dark. Every day cows were milked and stock fed. Winter had come, and it was very cold. And there was no wood on the prairie to keep the stoves going. "We're just gonna have to burn cow chips," I told Ben. "We're just gonna have to pick 'em up on the prairie."

We hauled water by sled from Mr. Heinrich's well. I told Ben how Floyd's smoking shoes had burned up our old sled. Father had built us another. It wasn't fancy. A couple of old heavy boards, each about ten feet long and sawed to slant up at the front, served as runners. Father had nailed enough boards crosswise to provide deck space for four wooden water barrels.

When Ben and I finished our chores at home, other families needed our help. Some of those people lay there miserably sick, unable to eat anything but soup. Others, like Father, would have fever one minute and chills the next. Father was the worst in our family.

"He's got yellow jaundice on top of the flu," Dr. Hansen told us wearily one afternoon. The young doctor looked like he had been sleeping in his rumpled blue serge suit. He left again almost at once to call on other families.

Mother was very worried about Father, having lost a child shortly after birth to influenza.

"Keep giving him plenty of that soda and vinegar," she whispered from her sickbed. "Don't let him push it away." That was the only medicine Dr. Hansen had recommended. On the prairie, it served as a standby for nearly everything.

April 1919 came, and Father was still sick, though all the others had recovered. But Father was stubborn and insisted on getting up to help with the chores, only to collapse and be carried back to bed, which was just as well.

An early -spring blizzard, one of the worst in Kansas history, struck our part of the state one day. The wind whistled across the treeless prairie, piling up huge snowdrifts. Those who lived far from Rolla, as we did, found themselves snowbound for several weeks.

On the second day of the big storm, Father called Raymond and me over to his bed. "Have you hauled extra water for the stock?" he asked weakly.

"We got some," Raymond answered.

"Some?" Father echoed. "You both get on out there, now!"

"Yes, sir."

Father looked helplessly past us to Mother, busy at her stove.

"This snow. Maybe it's too deep already to haul water."

"We'll take care of it," Mother assured him as he closed his eyes and lay back, exhausted. She motioned for us to leave.

"Wait," Father said, opening his eyes again. "The stock, have them put . . . put them all in the barn."

My brother and I floundered about in chest-deep drifts as we tried to chase the cows back toward the barn. They refused to go. They were milling about nervously, sending up clouds of fine snow that got into their eyes.

Raymond tripped and fell. He got up and went down again. The cattle were lowing now, getting edgier as they stomped about in their efforts to evade us. I saw Raymond fall again. When he got up, I saw him claw at his face with mittened hands.

"Glenn, I can't see!" My brother's cry reached me faintly above the whistle of the wind and the nervous mooing of the animals. I stumbled to Raymond's side. The snow was caked solidly over both his eyes. I tried to brush it free. I couldn't.

"It's frozen to your eyebrows!" I yelled into my brother's ear. "Here, take my hand. We're getting out of here."

However, we hadn't floundered a dozen steps together before my right leg suddenly gave out. We both went down. We struggled up and tried again. This time Raymond tried to help by letting me lean some of my weight against him. It failed, and we went down together again.

"If only I could see!" Raymond screamed helplessly.

"Just get up!" I yelled back. "I'll do the seeing."

Raymond had fallen on top of me. Now, as I pawed away the snow that clung to my face, I wondered how much longer *I* would be able to see.

"We're getting nowhere!" Raymond yelled as once more we got up, clinging weakly to one another. "I wish Father was here."

"We gotta think this through!" I shouted. I tried to think but couldn't.

A cow bumped into us, blinded by the snow and lowing unhappily. The cow's cold tail swung wetly against my face as it surged past.

Hey! Could it be? I wondered. *It has to be.*

I squinted in the direction the cow had gone. Through the swirling snow, I could see it. Barely visible, the cow was milling slowly about only a few yards away. I turned my brother so he faced in her direction.

"Move!" I yelled at him. "I got an idea."

The cow saw us coming and edged away. Holding on to Raymond with one hand, I eased past him and lunged at the cow. I managed to catch the end of her tail.

"Here, hang on!" I screeched, forcing the tail into my brother's hands. "We're goin' home."

With that, I whacked the animal hard on the flank. She obliged. Mooing loudly, she put her head down and moved slowly toward the barn. As she pulled us behind her, the other cows fell in step.

To reach the barn, the animals would have to pass our home. When the plodding cows came abreast of the house, I told Raymond to release his grip. Then, supporting each other, we staggered through the snow to the front door.

By the time we got there, we were both exhausted. I reached for the knob. It wouldn't turn. I tried to cry out, but I couldn't. Weakly, I tried pounding on it. Then my leg buckled. I collapsed, pulling Raymond down with me. We lay together on the snow-covered porch.

Where can Margerie be? I wondered vaguely. She had been in the house when we'd left. Had she decided to go to the barn to help Mother and Letha? *If she did, we're finished,* I told myself. Father was still too weak to get out of bed, and little Johnny and Melva didn't know how to open the front door.

Maybe we should have gone around to the back, I thought. *But that would have been so much farther. And we're so weak.*

It was too late now. I could feel Raymond reaching clumsily for my hand.

"They'll never find us in time," he mumbled in my ear, his words already thickening from the cold. "We're gonna die, Glenn. Right here at the front door."

His words seemed to reach me from afar. Somehow, it didn't seem to matter.

I regained consciousness with a start. I lay in a warm bed. Had the bitter blizzard been just a nightmare? No. But my right leg ached terribly. The pain went deep into the hip. I groaned and felt someone gently touch my face. It was Mother. She was bending over me, making little sounds of concern. It occurred to me that she had been doing the same thing when I had awakened in bed after the fire.

"How's Ray?" I exclaimed.

"He's all right. You're both gonna be all right."

"My leg's not all right. I wish it would get well and stay well."

She glanced away. Her soft gray eyes shared my concern.

Mother explained to Raymond and me what had happened. Margerie had not heard us at the door, but my dog, Jack, had. The little terrier whined and scratched against the inside of the door, and Margerie found us when she got up to let the dog out. She quickly pulled us inside, then ran through the swirling snow to get Mother and Letha, who had gone out the back door to deal with the cows.

Later, after Letha and Margerie had helped Mother carefully remove the melting ice from our eyelids, the girls managed to get all the stock safely into the barn, and we eventually got warm.

In the raw, cold days that followed, the endless prairie wind continued to shift the snowdrifts. Dr. Hansen reluctantly gave in to my father's impatient demands and allowed him to get out of bed for short periods.

"But only if you promise to remain indoors," he warned.

To soothe his restlessness from being cooped up in the house, we kids took turns playing checkers with him after chores. Sometimes we'd talk to him about what we'd learned in school that day.

6

My First Race

Father liked to talk to me about running. Before the fire, he had told me that I was a "natural."

"You got a good stride, boy," he observed once after I'd beaten my two older brothers in a race to the barn. His habit was to assign us boys handicaps as we all raced for the barn at daybreak each morning to feed the stock before school. He always reached the barn first, no matter how much of a head start he gave us. He could run like a deer.

Father had taught all of us, even Mother, quite a few things about running. Things like how to pump your arms to get more speed and how to pace yourself during a long run to save your wind for the final effort.

Father would never talk of it, but Ray and I suspected he might once have secretly wanted to be a professional runner. Still, if we asked him about it, he'd give a stern look of disapproval and warn us that displaying that kind of ability in public was "showing off."

Spring came. Many had died from the great flu epidemic. Father had been one of the lucky ones, but he remained thin and weak.

"You know, we've been renting this farm for four years now," Father announced quietly at dinner one night. Mother nodded. Father glanced about the table at the rest of us.

"Don't you reckon these young 'uns are ready for a change?" he asked. "Like moving to Elkhart to try some city livin'?"

Move! The word was exciting. Mother smiled as we all six squealed our approval. "But can we afford a place in Elkhart?" she asked.

He sighed. "I 'spect not."

Mother's smile faded. Father let us wait just long enough. Then a mischievous twinkle slid into his light blue eyes. "We're gonna live in a tent," he announced importantly. "A real big tent!" This time we youngsters squealed even louder.

That night, we kids found it hard to go to sleep in our upstairs room. Rolla had three hundred residents. Elkhart, twenty miles farther west in Kansas, had nearly two thousand people.

"It's got a fancy movie house an' everything!" Margerie whispered.

Father still owned the big covered wagon in which we had begun our westward migration. Now, once more, we loaded our possessions into it and a smaller farm wagon. Leaving Rolla and all its memories behind wasn't too difficult for us. So much had happened there—the fire, Floyd's death, and my still painful recuperation.

I regretted leaving Dr. Hansen, though. When I thought about it, he had been a patient, kind, and helpful physician who had seen our family through a most difficult time. I'd always be grateful to him.

Father had arranged for our tent to be set on the flat prairie about a mile beyond the Elkhart city limits. It was near a farm, the owner of which had given Father permission for us to use his windmill for water. Mother gasped when she saw the size of the tent.

"It's big enough for a circus!" she exclaimed. "Where in the world did you get it?"

"War surplus," he explained, delighted with her reaction. "Bought it real cheap, too."

The tent was square at its base, fifty feet on each side, and so heavy that Father had to hire two men to help us suspend it from its big center pole. The brown canvas sloped downward to form four walls, each five feet high. The sides were held out by stout ropes tied to hardwood stakes, which Raymond and I helped Father drive into the ground.

"Don't put any furniture where it might touch the canvas," Ray and I were cautioned as we carried things into the tent. The canvas might leak when it rained.

Our furniture wasn't fancy, but we valued what we had. We placed the brown enamel heater near the center. Mother's cook stove was near one wall where there was a reinforced hole in the canvas for the tin stovepipe. There were no closets. Personal things were in cardboard boxes under the beds or on the dirt floor. Our home had shrunk in size from two rooms to one.

"How will we take a bath?" Margerie asked.

Father grinned. "Same as before. In Mother's washtub. We'll just hang up some blankets to hide it."

We built an outdoor privy and used most of our garbage to feed the hogs and chickens. The rest we buried. The daily two-mile walk to and from school in Elkhart further strengthened my legs, but I still couldn't run without pain.

There were times when we kids didn't finish our farm chores on time. Then Margerie, Letha, and Raymond had no choice but to leave me trudging embarrassingly behind while they ran ahead to avoid being late for school. *I'll learn to run again*, I would promise myself as I watched them go. I even shouted after them one morning, "I'm gonna win races again!"

I walked home alone from school one day past an unsightly dumping place for old oil drums and other rusting refuse. I saw a rabbit hop suddenly into view from a roadside ditch. Stealthily I slipped into the ditch and crept toward the bunny.

A noise scared the rabbit, and it darted into my arms with the force of a hurled shot put. I managed to get my hands on it and stood up, holding the struggling bunny triumphantly by its ears. And then it happened: my weak right leg gave way as I tried to get out of the ditch. I fell backward and flung both arms wide to cushion my fall. The kicking rabbit fled.

I lay there, wanting to cry. *I'm just a cripple!* I told myself bitterly. *I can't even hang on to a little ol' rabbit.* How could I ever expect to run again?

That summer, we sweltered in the big tent. The sun beat down upon the heavy canvas, making it smell heavily of old oil. There were no windows for ventilation, and the only door was small. It was just a folded-back canvas flap.

Winter came, and it was not unusual to wake up and find powdery snow on the bedclothes. When the wind blew hard, the big tent would creak and groan. The walls vibrated at times with a loud humming sound that woke us all up. Sometimes a stake would pull loose from the sandy soil, and the wall on that side of the tent would begin to flap violently, letting the snow swirl in underneath.

Mother didn't complain about the heat or cold. However, she did protest Letha's starry-eyed announcement at dinner one evening.

"I think I wanna get married."

Dean Morgan was a local farmer's son, nineteen years old. A friendly, hardworking blond boy with a square face, he'd had dinner with us several times. Letha had met him in their junior class at Elkhart High. The noisy table grew suddenly quiet. Mother slowly put her fork down on the red-checkered oilcloth.

"Child, you're only fifteen," she declared, her voice strained. Father, too, had stopped eating.

Letha flushed. "Please, Mother. Lots of girls get married when they're fifteen."

Mother gave an impatient little shake of her head. The movement dislodged some of her graying hair. She brushed it back with a careworn hand as she stared at Letha. Letha turned helplessly to Father, but he just shook his head.

"You gotta be careful about this, honey," he told her gently. "It's for the rest of your life."

Tears came to Letha's big eyes. "Me an' Dean love each other," she wailed. "You *hear*?" She stood up quickly and ran to her bed.

Reluctantly, my parents allowed Letha and Dean to be married the following spring. After the wedding, Father acted unusually quiet.

"Reckon it's time to be movin' on again," he announced abruptly at dinner one evening. "We have been livin' in this tent more than a year now."

Mother took the news with her usual calm. "You have someplace in mind?" she asked.

Father kept his glance on the food before him. "Yeah, out west. Maybe somewhere in the Rockies."

Again we were on the trail, this time to spend a year in Colorado. For me, it was a respite from the prairie, the endless flat land giving way to mountains and valleys, forests, and a log cabin.

Within a few short months, the family was again at the mercy of my father's restlessness. He couldn't seem to settle down. Always there would be some reason to pull up again and move.

"We're goin' back to Elkhart," he told us one evening at supper.

"More money to be made back there farmin' than cuttin' timber here."

I was twelve by the time we returned to Elkhart. My father rented a small frame house on the city's outskirts and sold the covered wagon. It had carried the family and our belongings more than a thousand miles.

Although returning to Kansas wasn't what I wanted at the time, it would prove to be a turning point in my life. Our frequent moving had hindered our education, and that bothered my mother. We hadn't attended school in Colorado and had lost a full year.

Before that, we had lost still another grade because of the move from Rolla to Elkhart. Mother had purposely held us back for one year then, fearing that our studies would prove harder in the city school. And I had lost a third year when my legs had been burned. I promised myself I'd study hard and skip a grade to make up at least one of those lost years.

When I returned to school in Elkhart, I entered the fourth grade, still a small kid but tough. Hard work on the farm and the grueling effort to walk and run again had made my muscles like rocks. Then, for the first time in my life, I encountered a bully. He was a big heavyset kid, at least a head taller than I, who was always picking on younger, smaller children. One day on the playground before school, he abused a scrawny, freckled-faced little guy I had befriended. I warned him to stop.

"You gonna do something about it, Cunningham?"

I started after him, but the bell rang for us to go to class, and he quickly headed for the schoolhouse.

"Wait till after school, big guy; I'll get you then," I shouted after him. During class time, my anger cooled, and I wondered what I was doing going after such a large kid. Later, at recess, I stole a look at him. He avoided my eyes. And he was sweating. Then I realized a startling truth : he was afraid of me!

The thought staggered me. In a few seconds, the bully went from cocky arrogance to trembling blubber. What had caused this? Somehow he had sensed my righteous fury, and it had intimidated him even though I was much smaller than he.

School ended, and the bully hurried out of the classroom. It took me three blocks to catch up with him. He was running by then, panting, glancing back over his shoulder to see how close I was. I caught up to him and grabbed his shoulder. As he turned, I plunged my left fist into his stomach. He let out a grunt and fell backward. When he hit the ground, I was on top of him, punching him at will until he began to cry. I got up.

"Don't you ever pick on those little kids," I warned. "If you do, I'll get you again."

This victory over a bigger boy suddenly made me want to compete against the bigger kids in athletic competitions. On impulse, I decided to enter the school track and field meet the following week.

"I want to win that little medal they got on display in the drugstore window," I confided to a classmate. "The one for the mile run. It looks like it might be pure gold."

"Win? You?" he scoffed. "Don't be a fool, Scarlegs!"

Dr. Hansen had told me I would carry the huge, blue-black scars that had earned me my nickname to my grave. But my legs now felt quite strong despite several ugly places where the flesh had not grown completely back.

I was careful not to reveal my decision to enter the mile race at home. My parents still didn't approve of athletic events.

"If you youngsters ain't gettin' enough exercise from your chores, I can always have somethin' extra waitin' for you when you get home from school," I had once heard Father tell Floyd.

The race was scheduled for the following Saturday. That was the day of the annual farmers' fair. It was also the day of the week when my parents hitched the mules to our farm wagon to go into town for supplies. We kids usually went along since sometimes our parents bought us a few little things. If there was no money to be spent, we just window-shopped and stood around watching people. This time I stayed home. After my family had gone, I jumped on Beauty, my brown-and-white pony, and galloped bareback to the fair.

It was a clear, crisp morning when I arrived at the cow pasture at the edge of town. About a hundred people were already there, wandering between the small tent and wooden stands where homemade cakes, jellies, and other things were for sale. In the pasture, a man was pulling a road drag behind a team of horses.

"What's he doin' that for?" I asked someone.

"He's layin' out the racetrack. Cuttin' the grass off down to the dirt. It makes it easier for the runners."

"How far is it around that circle he's makin'?"

"Half a mile."

That meant I would have to go around twice. Mr. Simmons, the school principal, was the person I had to see if I wished to enter the race. I sought him out in the crowd.

"Do you intend to run like that?" the principal barked, letting his small black eyes focus impatiently on my homemade woolen shirt and pants, thick-soled canvas sneakers, and heavy socks.

"Yes, sir," I told him. This unsmiling, often threatening man was the only one of my teachers I didn't like. Mr. Simmons motioned me toward a nearby gathering of people where the entrants were weighed.

"You're so small you'll have to run in Class B races," he said shortly.

I wanted to run in Class A because that was where the shiny medal was the first prize. So I sauntered over to the Class A line and got in it.

"How much do you weigh, son?" the man at the scale asked when my turn came.

"How much you gotta weigh?" I asked warily. Several of the onlookers laughed.

"At least seventy pounds." The man must have seen the concern on my face as I stepped gingerly onto the scale. I was glad I had on my heaviest underwear. The weigh master hardly glanced at the reading. "Exactly seventy pounds!" he announced. "Who's next?"

Several shorter races were run before the mile. I let my glance wander apprehensively over to the swelling crowd as I waited. I thought if Father showed up, I'd surely get my bottom warmed. Finally someone yelled, "All runners in the Class A mile event line up at the starting line!"

I studied my competitors as they took their positions. There were eight of them, nearly all high school boys, and all were bigger than I. I was the only one not wearing running trunks.

I was startled when I looked at the feet of those giants. *These nuts!*

They have nails driven through the soles of their shoes! I thought. *They're gonna stick fast to the ground with every step they take!* I had never seen a pair of spiked running shoes. I had never even seen a public race.

"On your mark!" called the starter. From the corners of my eyes, I noticed that the others got down on one knee with both hands touching the ground. I did likewise. "Get set. Go!"

At the yell, the entrants jumped to their feet and took off fast. *Boy, look at those big guys fly!* I thought. I did not try to keep up with them.

Father had always told us kids to "save enough breath to get you there" when he raced us in long runs. One of the big pacesetters lasted only about a quarter mile. When I caught up with him, he staggered to the inside of the track and lay weakly panting on the grass.

I put on a little speed now. Soon I had passed several of the older boys. By the time we finished the first lap, I had caught up with the two front-runners. They pounded side by side, and I recognized one of them. He stood six feet four inches, and everyone expected him to win. I wanted to pass them.

I didn't know you were supposed to pass on the outer side of the track, so I just went right between them, ducking under their pumping elbows. The favorite glanced down in surprise.

"Pretty fast clip you're setting, bub," he growled at me.

Father had told us, "When you run, don't talk." So now I just looked up at this big guy and answered, "Huh?"

He repeated his comment.

"Huh?" I said again.

"Be careful," puffed the other. "He's so little you might step on him."

"Huh?" I asked.

They soon caught on and said no more.

I better start putting some distance between these fellows and me, or they'll sprint away at the finish, I told myself.

I pulled away from them. The next thing I knew, I came up to this string stretched right across the track. I saw that it would catch on my head, so I just ducked under it and kept on going.

New shouts came from the cheering watchers. Puzzled, I glanced back over one shoulder. People were waving for me to go back.

"Son, you gotta *break* that string to win!" one man yelled.

I whirled about and ran back as fast as I could. But it looked like I was too late. The other two runners were bearing down on that string.

Land! Am I gonna lose the race after winning it? I thought as I put on more speed.

7
Trouble with Father

The two big runners behind me had seen my mistake. As I furiously retraced my steps to break the tape properly, I saw them heading toward me like a pair of churning, snorting horses. Their chests were outthrust and heaving.

I imagined I could even hear the thudding of their spiked feet on the turf—a thudding that hammered into my brain as I tried desperately to reach that string.

Shoulder to shoulder, they came at me. Tears began stinging my eyes, mixing with the sweat running out of my hairline and down my forehead. My shirt and pants were soaked with sweat.

I'll never make it in time. Dimly I could see their massive forms coming closer. *Come on, Glenn, you've gotta do it!* Then another thought kept going over and over in my mind: *Better not run into them.*

The string was barely visible; I was more aware of it than seeing it as I reached out frantically and grabbed it. It snapped easily.

Within seconds the other two boys pounded past me. But I'd gotten there first! I'd won!

That medal was mine.

A roar of approval went surging up from the crowd. *That's for me!* I thought, dazed and bewildered. Then happiness washed over me as I realized that hundreds of people had just seen me win a race no one had thought I'd even finish.

And then I realized something else. I wheeled around and headed straight for Beauty, who was tethered nearby. I jumped onto her bareback, shouting to the surprised officials as I galloped away, "I'll pick up that medal on Monday."

I had to get home before my father did.

Beauty's hooves pounded a soft staccato on the hard ground as she carried me swiftly along the country roads back to our home at the edge of town. I felt a growing excitement rush through me as the full realization came: a little fourth grader had outrun those big high school guys from all over Morton County! I couldn't wait to get my hands on that shiny medal. Monday suddenly seemed a long way off.

I made it home first. The rest of the family followed a short time later.

And then, at last, it was Monday morning. This time, I got to school long before my brothers and sisters. Thirty minutes before classes began, I waited for Mr. Simmons in the school office adjacent to his own. I could see that medal hanging from my shirtfront. *I'll wear it all day and take it off before I get home*, I decided. All the kids would see it, but my father wouldn't. I'd have to figure out a way to tell him about it later.

The door opened, and in came gruff Mr. Simmons. He frowned when he saw me.

"What are you doing here, Cunningham?"

"Came to get my medal, Mr. Simmons. I won it in that race Saturday."

"I know, I know, boy. But I don't have it."

The words stopped me cold for a moment. "You don't have it? Where is it, then?"

"Got lost, Cunningham; it just got lost. Dunno how it happened, but we'll get you another one."

And he turned quickly and walked into his office. My shoulders slumped, and I wanted to cry. The thrill of victory had suddenly paled into emptiness. I didn't want another one; I'd raced for *that* medal, not a substitute.

As it turned out, I didn't even get the substitute.

What I did get was a whipping from my father that night when I got home from school and finished my chores. He'd learned of the race.

"You disobeyed me, boy," he said as he reached for the whip. "You knew how I felt about stuff like that racing in public. That's showing off, boy, nothing but showing off. I'm proud of you for winning, but I've got to punish you for disobeying."

The Cunningham children, c. 1911. Floyd, Raymond, Margerie, Letha. Glenn is in the front of Margerie.

Mrs. Wright's seventh-grade class in Elkhart, Kansas, probably spring 1924. Glenn is standing, back row, second from left.

Glenn running for the University of Kansas, early 1930s.

Glenn with two fellow KU athletes in front of boarding house in Lawrence, Kansas, early 1930s.

Glenn trains with Coach Bill Hargiss at KU, early 1930s.

Glenn and a young admirer, early 1930s.

Glenn, 1934.

Glenn with some of his teammates on board the ocean liner that took them to the Olympics in 1936. Glenn is just above the life preserver. To his immediate right are gold medal recipients Ralph Metcalfe and Foy Draper. Jesse Owens was Glenn's roommate.

Although Glenn didn't win the gold in the Olympic events, his teammates voted him Most Popular Man and presented him with this award.

Glenn with Kansas Relays officials, 1930s. University of Kansas sports legend James Naismith, who founded the game of basketball as well as the basketball program at KU, is at right.

At Madison Square Garden on February 23, 1935, Glenn established a new record for the 1500-meter run.

Glenn joined the US Navy in April of 1944 and was assigned as a physical fitness instructor. He served until June of 1946.

Mr. and Mrs. Glenn Cunningham. Glenn married Ruth Sheffield in 1947.

Glenn and Ruth at the Cunningham Youth Ranch, c. 1951. Glenn and Ruth ran the ranch for over thirty years, helping thousands of children.

Glenn in 1987. Photo by Don Tremain.

8

Herding Cattle

My fourth grade teacher, Mrs. Heueisen, made me aware of two impossible dreams. I was determined to achieve them both.

"Glenn," she told me one day, "you've got to get as much education as you possibly can. If you've got a good education, you've got security. Without it, you've got nothing. Always remember: education and security, they go together."

I began to yearn for education. I had no idea how I'd make it; I just knew I had to learn all I could remember in as short a time as possible. I was aware that I didn't want to be on the same treadmill as my father; he was in a trap from which there was no escape. I also was aware that I couldn't afford to aggravate him too much, or he'd pull me out of school to help full time with the farm work.

It was now 1923. With Floyd gone, only Raymond and I were left to help at home. John, my youngest brother, was only nine. I found myself doing all sorts of jobs to earn money for the family.

On weekends Ray and I collected garbage in Elkhart. We gave Father all our earnings from this and any other jobs we could find. Whenever I could, I worked for the cattle buyers who frequently rode through our area. They paid me to drive in cattle from outlying ranches to be shipped by rail from the Elkhart stockyard.

One Friday afternoon, a buyer who had heard of me called at the school. When my teacher brought me to the door, I could see that my runty size didn't impress him.

"How old are you, boy?" he asked.

"Fourteen."

"Them cows are thirty miles out. That ain't too far?"

"No, sir." I had driven herds many times that distance.

"There'll be one bull with 'em that's pretty mean."

"Yes, sir."

His voice sharpened. "The pay is a dollar and a half."

"Yes, sir."

After chores the next morning, I took my lariat and some food that Mother had given me and saddled up a little gray mule. "Here, better take this blacksnake, too," Father said. He handed me a nine-foot whip that he usually reserved for his own use.

When I arrived, the rancher pointed to a big black bull with sweeping horns. The hot-eyed animal stood inside an enclosure with the two dozen Hereford and Jersey cows I would bring to Elkhart with him.

"If that bull decides to come home, boy, you just let him," the rancher warned. "Ain't anybody been able to get him to the stockyard yet. Not even in a wagon with his legs tied." The rancher was a chunky man in overalls who always wore a big Stetson hat. The squinting eyes in his beefy red face never looked right at you when he spoke.

"I first tried to sell that bull as a two-year-old," he concluded, spitting on the ground. "He's four now."

"Yes, sir."

I had driven the small herd hardly a mile when the bull decided to return. He broke into a sudden run, long tail flying. I dashed after him on my little mule, but I didn't try to stop him. Instead, I just laid that blacksnake against his flanks as hard as possible. The mule helped. She dashed in repeatedly to bite the fleeing animal, her big, yellow-brown teeth crunching viciously on the big fellow's tail, each time right at the base.

It didn't take much of the whip and those teeth to change the bull's mind. He let us herd him back to the waiting cows.

Twice more that day, the bull tried to escape. The second time he tried, one of his long horns nearly gored my panting mule. I prepared to make camp at sundown beside a sturdy fence post that marked the corner of someone's abandoned pasture. I threw a loop over the unwilling bull's horns and tied him to the bar.

But that one-ton brute had other ideas. Snorting loudly, he just walked out to the end of my lariat, stretching it tight. Then he flipped his big head. The taut rope snapped like it was twine.

Then the bull turned to face me. He stomped one foreleg, eyeing me hotly. I stopped, stood very still, and stared back. The bull's hoof continued to paw up the dust, swirling it around onto its belly, eyes fixed in a glassy stare in my direction. Gradually the stomping slowed down. With a huge snort, he pounded the ground one last time, threw his head to one side, and strode back to the herd.

I knew it was no use to tie him up again; he'd snap the rope and do as he pleased. There was nothing to do but bed down for the night and see where he'd be in the morning.

Fortunately, he was still with the herd when I awoke. I got the animals underway, and throughout the day, the black beast gave me no trouble; he walked with the cows to the stockyard.

It was growing dark when we got there. Suddenly the bull dashed away between two long lines of cattle cars that stood in the big yard waiting to be loaded. When he came to an opening between the cars, he jumped through and ran away again in a new direction. My surefooted little mule managed to stay with him, biting his flank painfully whenever she got the chance. I kept flailing away with the big whip. Finally we got the bleeding, enraged bull into a pen, and I slammed the gate.

The following Monday, the seller was waiting when I was excused from school for lunch. "Boy, what did you use to bring in that bull?" he demanded, squinting at me suspiciously.

"Just a whip," I answered innocently. "A blacksnake and an old gray mule with big yellow teeth."

Occasionally, when I earned extra money like this, my father let me keep some to take my brothers and sisters to a movie in Elkhart. On this particular night, we saw a newsreel that showed Paavo Nurmi, the great Finnish runner, setting a new world record.

"I sure wish I could run like that!" I announced as we left the theater. Nurmi had run the mile in the incredible time of 4 minutes, 10.4 seconds.

Melva, my youngest sister, liked to tease me. "You couldn't have kept up with that feller on a bike, Glenn," she said.

"Someday I'm gonna break a record," I told her. "I betcha!"

"The only record you'll break is the one for feedin' hawgs," Melva shot back, and the others snickered.

That spring, Margerie told us that Bill Chamberlin, the farm boy she had been keeping company with, had asked her to marry him. They were wed shortly after that in a simple ceremony.

By summer, I had finished the sixth grade, and I entered junior high school that fall. Since Elkhart's educational system combined junior high and high school within the same building, I found myself able to participate in the athletic program there.

"Glenn," Mother told me when I informed her of my opportunity, "you know your father doesn't like public displays of that kind."

"It's part of the school program, Mother."

Elkhart High School had but one coach for athletics, and I got off to a bad start with him the first time I went out for track.

"Stay with that big feller until the last hundred yards," Coach Varney told me, pointing to a boy who held the school record for the mile. "When you're in the stretch, sprint and try to beat him if you can."

I didn't know what "stretch" meant, and I had no desire to reveal my ignorance by asking. The race began, and a half dozen of us got off to a good start. I was wearing running shoes for the first time in my life. The spiked, heelless shoes seemed to give wings to my feet. The champion was a strong boy who towered above me and ran with a powerful, pounding gait. But I noted that he slowed when the curving track brought us around into the wind. The wind wasn't bothering me, and long hours of field work had hardened my muscles. So I just sailed past the slowing champ.

I ran so fast that I broke the school record by 18.9 seconds. I felt sure the coach would be pleased. Instead, he was furious.

"Don't ever do that again," he shouted at me in front of the rest of the track team. "Don't you ever disobey me again, Cunningham!"

The coach refused to let me run another mile race for the rest of the track season as punishment.

Coach Roy Varney was a man in his late twenties. He was well-built and a good athlete himself. His voice was loud, often impatient when he instructed us. And at times, the dark brown eyes in his square face could look positively disgusted with us. Behind his brusque manner, however, I recognized a lot of knowledge. I made up my mind I'd learn from him.

9
Babe Ruth

For the first time, I learned that the standard running events are sprints of 100 and 220 yards, middle distances of 440 and 880 yards, and the 1-mile run. There are also relay races held between teams of four persons, each passing a baton to the next.

"Usually, track and field meets are held outdoors on oval, quarter-mile cinder tracks," the coach told us. "If a meet is held indoors, it is run on flat armory floors or on a specially constructed board track that can measure from eight to twelve laps to the mile."

The main sports-governing body in the United States is the Amateur Athletic Union (AAU). Organized in 1888, the AAU has jurisdiction over all track and field events.

"Break the AAU rules, and you're finished from then on in the amateur competition," the coach warned us. "Any runner who conducts himself in an unsportsmanlike manner or who competes for money or gets himself involved in anything dishonest will immediately lose his amateur status. The AAU will quickly see to that."

It was not unusual for Varney to become impatient with me. "Cunningham," he might yell, "get those legs stretched out! I want you to develop a long stride; don't run like a fire horse."

He was also unhappy with how my feet hit the ground.

"It's a rocking motion we want," he would explain, shaking his big head mournfully. "The heel hits first, followed almost at the same moment by the toe. Why do you persist in making two separate movements of it?"

I had no idea why. The coach focused on improving both my form and my attitude. He mentored my running career and shaped me so I could reach my dreams.

When winter set in and it became too cold for track events, I played basketball. When spring arrived, I played baseball. And when summer came and school was out, I worked in a grain mill. Time was passing quickly for me. I was very involved in athletics, studying hard and keeping my body in shape in any way I could.

In 1928, I suffered an injury that had a lasting effect on much of my career. During baseball practice, I was squatting behind the plate, catching without a mask, when the batter swung and only tipped the ball. But that ball was like a rock. It hit me right on the mouth. Since we had knocked the cover off it earlier and rewound the ball with friction tape, I could taste that tape mingled with blood from my badly bruised mouth. Eight teeth were knocked loose. Several days later, however, they seemed to be all right. When the swelling went down, I forgot about it.

After a summer of working in the mill, I was ready for school to start again. The coach had banned me from running the mile the previous year because of my disobedience. This year would be different. And I did get along better with my coach. He let me run in every event that our high school entered. I won them all.

But I've got to do even better, I kept telling myself. *I've got to become so good that people will tell my father to let me stay in school.*

My chance for this kind of recognition came when Coach Varney watched me unofficially break the world scholastic record for the mile run.

"I think it's time I took you to Chicago, Cunningham," he announced thoughtfully. "The best high school runners in the nation will be competing there."

Though still unconvinced about the importance of track competition, my father allowed me to go.

I'd never been to a big city, and Chicago fascinated me; I wanted to see everything. I walked around the city until my feet ached.

"How about a baseball game, Cunningham?" the coach suggested late one afternoon. The Yankees were in town, which meant Babe Ruth would be playing.

"Let's go!" I replied.

That night Ruth hit a home run, and its memory is still as vivid now as it was that night in 1928.

As we walked back to the hotel, I began limping.

"What's the matter, Cunningham?" Varney glanced at me, worry on his face. "Not your leg, is it?"

"Naw, just a blister on my heel. Too much walking around town, I guess."

"I wanna take a look at it when we get back to the room."

It was a bad blister. By morning I had a fever. An infection had set in during the night.

"Let's get you to a doctor," Varney said firmly.

"I'll be all right, Coach, really I will." Desperation was starting to creep over me; I had to be in that race the next day.

"We're going to a doctor, Glenn." His voice was even more adamant.

The doctor took my temperature: 104.5 degrees. He looked at the blister, which by now had swollen the entire heel and was an ugly black.

"You say this boy's supposed to race tomorrow?" He turned to Varney.

"He's supposed to, yeah."

"You can't let him run like this! It's impossible."

The coach stared at my bare, badly bruised heel for a moment. Then he looked me straight in the face.

"He's right, Glenn. I'm canceling you out tomorrow."

I was frantic.

"You can't do that!" I said hoarsely. "I just gotta run in this race."

"Sorry, Glenn."

I hopped down from the examining table and pulled Coach Varney aside. The doctor turned his attention to something else.

"Listen, Coach. My whole future could depend on this race. You just got to let me run."

He looked at me quietly, struggling inside. I knew he understood. "I do understand," he said finally. "I've had to work my way up from nothing, too, you know. All right; if you're better tomorrow, you can run."

I'd be better tomorrow, all right.

The following afternoon, Chicago's huge Stagg Field was crowded as I emerged from a dressing room and trotted out to the starting position with the other mile contestants.

I hadn't dared tell Varney how bad I was feeling. I was only vaguely aware of the big athletic field as a world of swimming color, yelling people, and intermittent snatches of blaring band music. The hot sun was making my fever worse.

At the starter's gun crack, I moved out fast, contrary to my usual procedure. I wanted to get it over with—before I fell on my face. The other contestants had the same idea, however. Several of them wouldn't let me get in front.

The winner of this race would be the best high school miler in the world.

I put on more speed, trying to ignore my throbbing head and my infected heel's excruciating pain. I was dropping back. *You can do it!* I assured myself. *You've beaten guys like these before.* But my tortured heel was killing me.

A runner pounded past me. Then another. *Come on, go after those guys.* I managed to catch up with two of them, going around on the outside. Then I drew abreast of another. But I couldn't keep it up.

One by one, they passed me again. Each time my heel hit the track, waves of pain shot through my ankle and into my leg. There was no way I could force that leg to do anything more than it was doing. I finished fourth.

I stumbled from the track and into the waiting arms of my anguished coach.

"Sometimes you're just too darn stubborn, Glenn," he scolded, supporting me back to the dressing room. "You better change that 'I-can-do-it-my-way' attitude of yours. If you don't, it's going to cost you big someday."

When I returned home, my family offered no sympathy. When I showed them my blistered heel, not even Mother gave me care. They could be like that. Neither Father nor Raymond asked me why I'd lost the race.

I knew I would not disobey my father if he ordered me to quit school. To discourage the possibility, I found new work to do about the house at every opportunity when I wasn't helping with the farm chores. I worked twenty hours a day, sometimes more. I paid Father for room and board.

That summer, I worked at Jim Heintz's mill in Elkhart again. I was making good money now, nine dollars a day. Mother felt that I deserved to keep some of it, and Father agreed. I opened a bank account of my own.

The following fall of 1929, I was twenty and somewhat old to be starting my senior year in high school. Still, when Coach Varney announced , "We're going back to Chicago, Cunningham. Take care of yourself this time, and let's see if we can come back a winner," my stomach suddenly fluttered. More than anything else, I wanted a chance to redeem myself at Stagg Field. The heel was completely well.

The air seemed saturated with electricity that day.

The crowd was alive and filled the stadium, and I was in good shape as we lined up at the starter's post.

The gun sounded, and we were off. Studiously, I made certain I did everything as I'd been taught. I let several of the more eager runners get out ahead but kept a good pace to ensure that when my second wind came this time, I'd be ready to make my move.

The field of runners was good. These were high school students from throughout the country, the best the United States had to offer. The pace was fast, but this time I was ready for it. As the stretch came, I knew deep down that the moment had come. My stride widened, and my pace quickened. I felt myself glide by the front-runners, moving from fourth to third to second and into the lead.

I could see the tape up ahead; the red band stretched across the track, marking the finish. I wasn't aware that I was running fast, but I could hear the crowd's roar. Out of the corners of my eyes, I could see people standing, thrusting their fists into the air, and urging me on. I was setting a new world record for the interscholastic mile.

The tape broke as I chested it in full stride. Panting, I walked back to where Coach Varney was standing.

"Cunningham!" he screeched at me, his face one massive grin. "You did it. You broke the world record for a high school runner." He grabbed me in a huge bear hug.

The citizens of Elkhart were just as enthusiastic. When we returned, a band played, and people cheered as my parents and I rode down Main Street in the city fire truck. One of little Elkhart's high school students had broken a world record. It was a victory for the entire town since the people of Elkhart had collected the money to pay for Coach Varney and me to travel to Chicago, making it possible for me to participate in the track meet. Several big colleges telegraphed offers of scholarships.

Father hated all that fuss! During the victory banquet that followed, he wore a frozen smile. When the mayor insisted that he come to the microphone and say a few words, Father shook his head several times before reluctantly going forward.

"Mr. Cunningham, I know how proud you must be of this wonderful boy," the mayor announced. "I'm sure you must all be looking forward to the running records Glenn will set when he goes to college next year."

Father managed a weak smile, followed by a few brief thanks. He was wearing his only suit. I hadn't seen that old gray suit since Floyd's funeral. Melva, my youngest sister, grinned and made a face when I reminded her of my prediction that I'd break a record.

"Aw, you may win these little ol' kid races," she said flippantly, "but not the big ones like Nurmi does."

I had set my record by running the mile in 4 minutes, 24.7 seconds. Paavo Nurmi's record was 4:10.4.

Times were better for our family now. Father bought a small frame house in Elkhart. It was only the second property he had owned since my birth. He also purchased a gleaming black Model A Ford, our first automobile. It had isinglass side curtains that snapped fast to the canvas top. The isinglass was stitched with white thread to shiny black leatherette material that continued to smell new for a long time.

"You'll learn to drive it," Father told Mother, grinning.

"I'll stick with the mules," she replied.

Mother's health had been gradually failing. Hardly a day passed that she wasn't "all worn out," as she'd put it with a pale smile. We didn't discover why until one weekend when a bad dust storm descended on Elkhart.

There had been some warning this time, and the schoolteachers, anticipating that the children would be safer at home, excused us early that Friday afternoon. As I ran home, I knew what to expect. Overnight, dust and sand from a big storm could cover stock, fences, farm machinery—everything. After one of our screeching Kansas storms, I found a straw driven deep into a heavy piece of wood.

When I got home, I found my parents busily wetting bed sheets. These were hung hopefully over the tightly shut windows' inner surfaces to keep the dust out.

"Glenn, hustle out to the barn and help Raymond cover up the car engine," Father ordered. The wind could blow grit into the innermost parts of any piece of machinery. Melva and Johnny had already fastened wet handkerchiefs over their noses and mouths to better protect their lungs from the dust.

For two days, the storm raged. Our home shivered from the force of it. Despite our efforts, the dust seeped in. It spread over everything. It made our food taste gritty.

The second evening, seated at dinner, Mother had a violent coughing spell. I had noticed that she'd often coughed during this particular storm. But now her eyes closed in pain as she clutched her throat and retched noisily into her napkin.

Father was on his feet at once. He hurried to Mother's end of the table and slid a strong arm about her small shoulders. Gently, he took the napkin from her and looked inside.

We all stared fearfully at the black spittle there. We knew what it meant. After the storm, a doctor confirmed our fears.

"Your wife has dust pneumonia," he told Father. "She will die if you don't move her away from these dust storms." This blunt Kansas doctor had seen many people die from dust pneumonia. After the doctor had gone, Mother tried to raise our spirits.

"Oh, it can't be that urgent," she said, smiling slightly. "We know that it can take years before you die from it." We didn't agree with her.

"Father, you can have the money I've been putting in the bank for college," I told him impulsively.

The next morning, I went to school as usual. The teacher's first words to us that day still live vividly in the minds of millions who recall the autumn of 1929.

"The stock market crashed yesterday, students. We should spend some time discussing what this means to our country. I think our nation will soon be in the grip of a very great economic depression."

I wasn't quite sure what she meant. A few minutes later, I understood a lot better.

"The banks have closed," she continued. "I understand no one can deposit or withdraw money. It will be hard now to buy food, pay bills . . ."

But I wasn't hearing her anymore. *I have to get to the bank! They have to let me get my money out. Mother's life might depend on it.*

Abruptly, I got up and walked out. When I reached the front door, I broke into a run. When I got to the bank, I confirmed the teacher's information: it was closed. Angry people were milling about outside.

Father, like other farmers in our area, was put in a critical financial position. And with Mother ill, he needed my help more than ever. College next year now seemed out of the question.

My teacher didn't agree. "Scholarships will continue," she said. "You can get most of your expenses paid."

I shook my head. "When people give you something like that, they think they own you," I replied. "I don't want to be obligated."

"This is no time to act independent, Glenn."

"I'll find a way to go to college. You wait and see," I assured her.

The banks opened again, but the depression worsened. The mill shut down and remained closed during the summer harvest season. Jobs were almost impossible to get. I found work only because I was willing to do anything, day or night. I was offered a job that Ray and I had held some years before.

Mother's health worsened. She could no longer do the neighbors' laundry. Our combined family income didn't pay all the bills. Father put our home up for sale, but no one had the money or desire to buy it.

Meanwhile, Melva married Loren Sitton, a husky local boy. They moved to Idaho. And I decided to leave, too.

There was a hurt look in Father's eyes when I told him my decision. I had decided to go to Lawrence, Kansas, to attend the University of Kansas. But I would not accept a scholarship; that seemed like charity. I would pay my way.

"What makes you think this is best for the family?" Raymond asked as he drove me to the railroad station. "How you figure you're gonna help Mother by running in college races? Didn't you say that amateur athletes aren't allowed to accept payments?"

"That's true. But I'll find a way to help you all." I had given my parents everything I'd earned that summer. After I purchased my train ticket, I had $7.65 left.

"I need a job," I told the university track coach when I arrived.

"Everybody needs a job," Coach Brutus Hamilton replied impatiently. But he promised to see what he could do.

I liked the large campus at the University of Kansas. I had run several times in meets there, and I remembered the pretty campus trees and the birds and squirrels that played in them. I found an attic room nearby in a three-story boarding house. The ten-dollar weekly rent included three daily meals. I managed to convince the skeptical landlady that I'd be able to pay her.

The coach found me a job. "You'll have to clean the stadium after football games and see to it that the players' uniforms are kept clean," he explained. I would be paid forty cents an hour.

"I'll do it," I told him. To get my coveted education, I was willing to launder jockstraps. I would find additional ways to earn and save money.

I also had a new challenge: I had a reputation to live up to; after all, wasn't I the world's fastest high school miler? Like my family members, the students at the university were waiting for me to do something spectacular.

They would wait a while. To my disgust, my scarred legs started hurting again. At times they hurt almost as much as they had while I was recovering from the fire.

"You're in no shape to work out, Cunningham," Coach Hamilton snorted one afternoon as he watched me attempt to run. He ordered me to pay a visit to the university doctor. I did.

"I can't find anything seriously wrong, son," the doctor said. "You do have a weak transverse arch in your left foot, but that shouldn't cause discomfort in both legs."

Unfortunately, he didn't think to send me to a dentist for X-rays of those teeth that had felt the baseball's impact.

The leg pains continued to mystify the coach and me. The pains could be excruciating one day, then gone the next. One thing was certain: cold weather caused the muscles in both legs to become stiff and sore. That winter, I did almost nothing on the track.

I did talk Coach Hamilton into letting me compete in the telegraph meets. Later, when the various college athletes' best running times were compared by telegraph, he discovered that the University of Kansas had won the Big Six Conference. I had run the mile faster than anyone else despite my aching legs.

My mother's health was always on my mind. I was scrimping, sending home every penny I could. Father no longer had Raymond to help him. My older brother had married a very pretty girl, Virgie Hargiss, and moved to Idaho to cut timber. I wished we could move Mother to that healthier state, too.

During my sophomore year at Kansas University in 1931, my legs felt better. Perhaps receiving a challenge helped. There was a senior at Iowa State who was "simply unbeatable," according to the sportswriters. They said it took him "another quarter mile just to slow down" after crossing a finish line.

One day Coach Hamilton told me with a grin that this other miler had issued a personal challenge to me. "He says he's gonna beat you so badly you won't even finish on the same side of the track with him."

I accepted the challenge, but I was worried. My coach wasn't. On the day of the race, his instructions were simple. "I'll be standing at the first turn," he said. "I'll motion to you whether I want you to move out or lay back."

Coach Hamilton let the other boy carry the first lap. I didn't mind. My legs might start hurting at any moment.

The coach motioned for me to lead during the second lap. I did, and he waved me out front for a repeat performance on the third. Then even faster on the fourth. I thought, hopefully. *Surely he'll let me drop back now.* But Hamilton just kept motioning me on faster and faster.

When I began the eighth and last lap, he signaled me to give it everything I had and start my sprint toward the finish line.

My legs were still feeling good, and I came off that turn as fast as possible. When I did, the crowd just stood up and roared. *Land!* I thought. *Here he comes!*

I sprinted on, driving with my arms. I pounded that track with everything in me. It was no use. I could hear the *pat-pat-pat* of his feet coming up on me.

The cheering watchers went wild when it came time to make the last turn and enter the straightaway. *It's going to be awful close*, I realized as I gritted my teeth and gave with every ounce of strength I had left.

I failed to pull away from him. I could still hear that relentless *pat-pat-pat*. I knew he must be right at my shoulder!

With one final effort, I broke the tape. Wearily I turned to shake hands with my challenger. And then I stared. The other boy was still on the other side of the track. I had been hearing the piece of numbered paper that the racing officials had pinned to the back of my shirt slapping in the wind as I ran.

My challenger learned a lesson about arrogance: he finished in the exact position he had boasted he would leave me in. I heard no more from him.

10
KU and the Olympics

In 1932, Bill Hargiss was named the new track coach at the University of Kansas, and we became close friends. He recognized my abilities as a runner. As a result, he decided to spend more time with me as a coach and friend. We began sharing our feelings, things like how we felt about athletics, how it felt having to overcome the awful pains of disability, and even how we felt about living in the United States. I told him about Floyd's death and the terrible times growing up on the Kansas prairie.

"Someday I'd like to do something that would let the whole world know how much I love our country," I said to Coach Hargiss one day.

"Real patriot, aren't you?" he said jokingly.

"Yeah, I guess I am," I replied. "But where else could a poor farm kid have the chance to do the things I've done?"

"I'm glad you feel like that," the coach said. "Maybe you'll get the chance."

"What do you mean?"

"I've thought you should try out for the Olympics."

"The Olympics!" That was the dream that had fed my imagination when I'd first run in the fourth grade: I'd aim to win the 1500-meter run, a distance only slightly shorter than the mile.

"Why not?" my coach countered. "Sure, you'll have to run in the collegiate regionals before you'll be able to compete at the Olympics, but it's certainly worth a try." And so we began the rounds of the collegiate regional competition, during which I got to know a young runner named Jesse Owens, who I felt had great potential.

As the coach and I traveled about by train, our expenses paid by the University of Kansas, I often skipped meals, sending the money home instead.

"I don't like that, Glenn," Coach Hargiss told me one day. "You need your strength, and one of the ways you get that is by eating properly."

"It's better that I send the money home," I replied. "My family needs it more. Anyhow, I'm winning everything I enter, aren't I?" And I was. Even in the national eliminations, I won it all.

And then it was time to go to Chicago and the Olympic tryouts.

My first test would come against other runners who had survived the national eliminations. It was a qualifying heat, and I won that, too.

My success meant that I'd represent the United States in the 1500-meter event at the 1932 Olympics. When the coach told me, I was awed. I would be carrying the colors of my country.

We took the train to Los Angeles for the Olympic track and field events. Then it happened: before the race, I woke up with a throat so sore I could hardly speak. The coach rushed me to a doctor who examined me carefully.

"Infected tonsils," he said laconically. "I'll give you some pills, but I want you to bed rest for a couple of days. If the infection doesn't clear up, you'd better have them taken out."

"I didn't come out here to go to bed," I said hoarsely. "The tonsils can come out after I run."

The doctor shrugged. "You won't have the strength to run."

My coach was nervous. "Glenn, you wouldn't listen to the doctors once before," he reminded me, "and you lost that race."

"Well, I'm not going to lose this one," I assured him.

There were over 100,000 people in the coliseum on that clear, sunny California day. A red-white-and-blue stripe slanted across the front of my jersey. In the center of that stripe was the flag of my country. I would run as I never had before.

On the first lap, my breathing became choked and agonizing pain appeared in my chest. Although I led at the first turn, I was fourth by the time we hit the finish. Luigi Beccali of Italy won the gold medal. I was left gasping for air.

There would be no medal, no award, and no recognition for my Olympic effort—only failure. To make me feel even worse, I had beaten Beccali's winning time on several earlier occasions.

I had expected that my Olympic loss would cause the public to turn away from me in disgust. Instead, as I continued to win college races in the years that followed, running whenever my legs would permit it, I received thousands of letters from many nations, most of them from young people. I answered every one in longhand, always encouraging them to live a disciplined, honest, clean life. "Whatever you attempt, never quit," I'd encourage them.

A newspaper got hold of one of these letters, and soon I became "Mr. Clean": the young athlete who had promised his mother he would never drink, smoke, or bring embarrassment to his family. At the time, I accepted the label. It was the truth. In a way, honesty, discipline, and clean habits were my gods. I believed in God but gave Him no credit for helping me through my troubles. As far as I was concerned, my success was all due to my own efforts and endurance, to gutting it out through all the hardships. Later, I found out that God had always been by my side.

In the years that followed, many more triumphs came my way. I served as captain of the US track team that toured Europe in 1933 and the Orient in 1934. In 1934, I set two more records: the 4:08.4 indoor mile record in Madison Square Garden and a new outdoor mile record of 4:06.7 at Princeton, New Jersey, in an invitational meet.

I had achieved my boyhood dream and beaten Paavo Nurmi's world record. I even received a telegram from him congratulating me.

Meanwhile, I built up a solid, growing bank account, working at several jobs and saving part of my athletic travel allowance whenever possible. At night, I sometimes sat up in a coach instead of using a sleeping car when I traveled by train. I might go a whole day without eating to save my meal allowance.

I helped my father buy a small ranch in Idaho. After they'd moved out there, Mother's dust pneumonia began to improve. By then, Raymond and his wife, Margerie and her husband, Melva and her husband, and John lived in Idaho. It was a time that brought the family close together again.

There was a family tragedy, too. My brother Raymond, the once snow-blinded boy with whom I had survived one of the worst blizzards in Kansas history, was killed in an auto accident at Bonners Ferry, Idaho.

Once again, my big goal was the 1936 Olympic games in Germany. I qualified as one of the US entries for the 1500-meter run. I wanted to show the world that I could do much better than I'd done four years before.

On board the ocean liner that carried the US team to Europe was my friend Jesse Owens, the tremendous Black athlete. Jesse would win four gold medals at this Olympics, going down in history as one of the greatest athletes the United States had ever produced. I was Jesse's roommate at the Olympics, and we became lifelong friends.

The games were held in Berlin from August 2 to 16. Adolf Hitler, who had become chancellor only a few years before, was determined to make this event a showpiece for German power. Berlin became a massive citadel of pomp, parades, and parties.

My most vivid memory of Berlin was the weather: damp and cold. My legs became stiff as soon as I arrived, and, still not understanding the reason for these aches, I attributed them to my injuries from the schoolhouse fire.

The tension was palpable. Over five thousand athletes from fifty-three nations were there to compete in nineteen events. Coaches worked feverishly in the few days before the August 2 opening to make certain their teams were as close to physical perfection as possible; everyone was aware of the intense rivalry between the German and US squads. The pressure mounted almost by the hour.

Opening day finally arrived, and once more, the colorful Olympic flag flew high, and the symbolic torch flamed from a stadium wall. The torch had been lit by the sun's rays at Olympia, Greece, and been carried to the site of the games by a relay of runners. When necessary, ships and planes carried the ignited torch.

One by one, the athletes ran the shorter races. Then it was time for the so-called metric mile, which spanned 1,500 meters. I held the record for the American mile, and Luigi Beccali, the Italian who had beaten me so handily four years before, carried the Olympic best. We qualified along with ten other runners. We'd be running three and three-fourths laps around the 400-meter oval track in the massive new stadium.

As we took our places at the starting line, the crowd began to roar.

The 1500 meters was one of the major running events, and the massive crowd had been looking forward to it since the opening ceremonies.

The gun sounded, and the twelve of us leaped forward, the familiar butterflies of initial nervousness melting into the heat of competition.

At the start, there was some confusion as runners jostled one another for a position. But I was used to this, and I lay back, moving to the outer edge of the pack, running easily and waiting for an opening.

The crowd was noisy. I knew they wouldn't be yelling like that for long. They would be applauding the winners and forgetting the losers in less than four minutes, but I was not going to lose. At twenty-seven, this could be my last chance to prove myself.

The crowd's noise throbbed in my ears, modulated by my pounding heart. I was pouring on the power when my legs began to hurt.

Panic. Again, the pain, the aching, took hold of me. *Would it never go away?*

Dirt was striking my face, spurting up from the pounding track shoes of a blond German runner with thick legs. I put on more speed and went around him. I had my second wind now. I picked up the pace still more, this time passing several runners, including a guy named Jack Lovelock of New Zealand.

A swift Frenchman took the lead at the halfway point in the race. I decided to overtake him. I was about to pass the man when my right leg suddenly buckled! I nearly fell. I recovered at once, but now new pains stabbed my legs.

Once more I started after the Frenchman. This time I passed him, and the crowd went wild. I had the lead! The pace had become grueling. My eyes smarted, and my tongue felt dry and thick. *But listen to that crowd!*

We were in the stretch now. I lengthened my stride, fighting the pain. I pumped my arms harder.

But I was in trouble. Big trouble. My legs could give out completely at any instant.

I could see the finish line. I could also see the runner inching up on my right side. That fellow was passing me. The crowd went into a frenzy as I managed to pull away from him, but my legs were on fire. The realization enraged me.

It seemed so unfair. The anger gave me new strength as I pounded the cinders.

And then, too late, I saw that I wasn't going to make it. In the final lap, Jack Lovelock came out of nowhere.

From the corner of my right eye, I saw him launch into a mighty last effort. Jack crossed the line first. I finished second, capturing the silver medal, my first and only Olympic podium.

Later, as the reporters descended upon us, I made no mention of the leg pains. When a well-known sportswriter pressed me for a statement, I told him truthfully, "I feel I ran a fast race. I broke the world record for the 1500 meter. Only one person in the world ever ran faster."

The top five in that race had all broken the record. I was part of one of the greatest races in Olympic history.

In one way, the Berlin Olympics were the climax of my running career. While I continued to compete for five more years, winning many races and even setting the world indoor record for the mile in 1938, that silver Olympic medal in 1936 was a major turning point in my life. It was both victory and defeat. It made me realize that sports competition is valuable in many ways but never an end in itself. It began in me a time of self-examination.

What had all my victories accomplished? Those medals and trophies: did they have any significance other than making good decorations for my hall bookcases? Americans put athletic heroes on pedestals while they win, then quickly take them off when they lose. The adoration can be so temporary.

All those mile races had molded and shaped me into the kind of person who should have a positive influence on society, but how? What did I want out of life? Certainly not money.

After I retired from active racing and was offered $100,000 a year to do public speaking, I turned it down. I had earned enough money to buy sizable pieces of land, and my savings had accumulated. The funds would never answer my inner restlessness.

The "Mr. Clean" label that had been pinned on me was now embarrassing. Who could live up to all that it implied? I prided myself on my disciplined habits and didn't hesitate to state my convictions in public appearances. Still, a marriage that failed shortly after World War II convinced me that I was as fallible as other human beings.

One obvious direction to go was teaching. While I was running, I had taken education courses as an undergraduate at the University of Kansas; obtained my master's at the University of Iowa; and attended New York University, where I'd earned a PhD. In 1940, I accepted a good position setting up the health center at Cornell College in Iowa and later became director of athletics, health, and physical education.

Along the way, I made a discovery. It happened in the office of a dentist. As he examined my mouth, he exclaimed, "Glenn, all your front teeth seem to be dead. I'd better x-ray them." They were badly abscessed, and the dentist was astounded. "With all that poison pouring into your system through the years, it's a wonder you could walk, much less run."

The bad teeth were the same ones that had been knocked loose years before by the baseball wrapped in friction tape. No wonder I had so frequently suffered pain during my running career.

In 1944, I entered the US Navy, taking my basic training at the Great Lakes Naval Training Center and then going to Princeton University for officer training. Later I was assigned to the naval base at San Diego as a fitness instructor.

My time in the Navy gave me many opportunities to visit hospitals and talk to men who were battle casualties. Some of them, like me, had been badly burned. In a way, it was reliving my early experience in the schoolhouse fire all over again. When a few indicated that they were ready to quit on life, I offered emotional support and motivation as I shared my story with them.

11
The Youth Ranch

After my US Navy discharge, I bought a small house in Emporia, Kansas. One summer day in 1946, I was walking through my neighborhood when I ran into an old acquaintance.

"Ruth Sheffield, what are you doing in Emporia?" I asked.

The young woman smiled at me. "I have an uncle who lives here. He's a concert pianist, and I'm taking lessons from him."

Ruth had been one of my students at Cornell College before the war and may have been the first woman to graduate from Cornell with a degree in physical education. An outdoor girl, she had greatly impressed me with her vitality and adventuresome spirit. Her light gray eyes smiled at me through glasses with narrow black rims. Ruth still wore her dark hair in a college-girl bob, but she had matured into a lovely adult.

"You enjoy horses," I remembered. "Would you like to ride?"

"I'd love it!"

"How about now?" I invited.

She laughed. "In a skirt and high heels?"

"I won't look if the horse won't."

"Some other time. I promise."

Ruth and I often rode together after that. She was thirteen years younger than I and had been teaching school for the past two years. I discovered that we had much in common. Ruth became the only one of my acquaintances who could help me forget, at least temporarily, the aimless life I was leading.

While Ruth and I talked about the future, she asked me what I wanted from life. I talked about doing some teaching, handling my property, and accepting various speaking dates, but I could tell it was an unconvincing answer.

"Glenn, did you ever ask God what He might want you to do with your life?"

"No."

"But you said you believed in God, Glenn."

"Yes, I've always believed in God."

"Yet He's not very real to you."

I nodded. The conversation was getting uncomfortable. Ruth was much more religious than I was, and while I liked this quality in her, I didn't care to talk about my beliefs. I guess I was like my father in that respect. A lot of his secretive nature had been passed on to me.

"If you don't mind, Glenn, I'm going to start praying that God will open up for you a new work that will give your life more meaning."

It wasn't long after that conversation that Ruth and I became aware that more and more of the neighborhood children were hanging around my house. I had always attracted children. Some came because they had read about me. I made them welcome because I enjoyed young people's honesty, freshness, and limitless vitality. Sometimes Ruth and I would take a dozen of them to ride with us over the prairie. When we played sandlot baseball, Ruth would hit and run with the best of us. My bothersome legs had not given me any trouble since the dentist had removed the bad teeth.

The summer passed far too quickly. It all came to a head one evening when Ruth and I dined in a quiet little restaurant that had become a favorite.

"Glenn, I am thinking of taking another teaching position," she announced soberly.

I hated to think of being alone again. "I'm afraid that if you go, we won't see each other anymore," I told her.

Ruth reached across the table and gave my arm an affectionate squeeze. "You'll still have all those wonderful horses!"

"Honey," I burst out, "I don't want you to go."

Ruth blushed, but her glance clung to mine. At that long moment, we both knew that she would not go. We were married early the following summer.

Life began to take on meaning with this warm, wonderfully

impulsive woman as my wife. Ruth never seemed to tire of how I encouraged needy children to crowd into our home.

"Know something?" she teased. "I think you would have made a great kindergarten teacher."

"I've always loved kids," I admitted. "I've always wanted a dozen of my own."

"Well," she said with a smile, "we'd better get busy, then."

We did. Three sons were born in as many years. I greeted each one with the proud observation, "He's a Cunningham, all right."

And Ruth invariably sighed and replied, "That's for sure. The same big ears, bullet head, everything."

My new wife, I soon discovered, was hard to predict. A banker's daughter, Ruth had lived in a comfortable home in a small town where she'd led a very sheltered life. So I could only smile one day when she announced abruptly, "Glenn, we've just *got* to find a bigger place if you plan to continue playing second father to all these kids."

"It's only crowded in the summer," I reminded her. "And it's fun, isn't it?"

"It's fun," she agreed. "But these kids need more than that."

What's she leading up to? I wondered as she removed the black-rimmed glasses and polished the lenses on her apron. Ruth did that when she was concerned about something. She regarded me soberly.

"These youngsters need help," she said firmly. "And that means giving them more than just some good food and a place to sleep. I've been thinking about that big ranch of yours at Cedar Point. The one with the big house."

"That old place?" I protested. "It would take a lot of repairs before you'd want to live there. Besides, we've got it rented."

"I know. I've checked the tenant's lease. It expires soon. And, from what I saw, it wouldn't be difficult to restore the buildings. Glenn, you've been looking for work that would give more meaning to your life. This could be it."

"You sure have been doing some thinking, haven't you?"

"Yes, and praying." Ruth paused as a thoughtful look came into her eyes. "Remember how that place looked when we saw it shrouded in morning fog? That eleven-room main house with its cupolas and sharp-slanting roofs looms up from the prairie like a fairyland castle. Kids love to live in an atmosphere like that."

I remained skeptical. But I gave in to Ruth's plea that we at least make a return visit "so we can ride through those lovely big pastures again."

We placed our three little boys in the station wagon and trailered a couple of saddle horses behind us as we drove the thirty-five miles to our destination. Eight miles outside the little Kansas town of Cedar Point, our isolated ranch sprawled on rolling prairie. Tall maple trees stood on both sides of the long entrance drive. At the far end was the T-shaped, large, two-story frame house that had impressed my wife. A wealthy farmer had built it sixty years earlier. Clustered about the main eleven-room building were a five-room tenant house, a big barn, and several smaller buildings.

We found the tenant's wife waiting and chatted briefly with her. Then, leaving the children, Ruth and I mounted the horses and cantered away. Two fine streams ran through the property, and we followed one of these back into a pasture that extended for nearly a mile.

"Just look at the *room* kids could enjoy here!" Ruth squealed back at me over her shoulder as she broke into a happy gallop. She raced me to the crest of a grassy hill that overlooked the ranch spread out below. She reined in smartly and slid from her horse to wait for me. When I joined her, she slid an arm affectionately about my waist.

"Glenn, let's move here," she said softly, looking beautiful with a flushed face and windblown hair. "I've watched you. Helping needy youngsters has come to mean a great deal to you."

She's right, I realized. *I've never been so happy as I am here.*

Once we had settled our sons and ourselves into the big house, we began restoring it. We modernized the kitchen, repaired leaks in the roof, replaced broken windowpanes, papered walls, and repainted woodwork. At Ruth's suggestion, we had the big home's already spacious living room combined with the dining room, creating a large recreation area for youngsters. Ruth saw that divans and easy chairs were positioned invitingly about the walls. We provided sleeping quarters for girls on the first floor, where Ruth and I had our bedroom.

The boys would sleep in upstairs bedrooms with four bunks installed in each.

We also renovated the tenant's house. "Just in case we have an overflow of guests," Ruth explained.

I still received many invitations to give inspirational talks to schools, service clubs, and churches. I decided to accept some of them. I would tell my listeners that the "Cunningham Youth Ranch" had come into existence, and its doors were wide open to needy children. And at no charge. It staggers me how little planning and thinking I gave to this project that would involve thirty years of my life. But we were protected. Perhaps it went back to the day before the first children arrived, when Ruth and I talked through one phase of the program we would offer.

"The first need these youngsters have is for self-discipline," I stated. "They don't learn it at home; at least not many do, so we'll have to teach them."

"Self-discipline is important, I certainly agree," Ruth said, "but they also need spiritual teaching. They need to know the Bible."

"Who will teach them?"

"We will."

And we did.

12
One Man's Efforts

Over the years, I became less dependent on myself and more dependent on God. It didn't happen right away, but it did happen. It had to happen if our work with young lives had any lasting effect.

During the next thirty years, thousands of youngsters found a haven at the Cunningham Youth Ranches operated by Ruth, me, and our children (eventually, we had ten of our own). This work gave fulfillment to my life. All that I had learned in the running, the discipline, the persistence, the frugal living, and bearing the pain was shared with and taught to young people.

I love these youngsters and have a burning passion for seeing them win over inner weakness and loose morals. This victory is the ultimate challenge for all of us. Despite the obstacles thrown up by the world, we can testify from our years of experience that this inner victory is the biggest and the toughest to achieve.

It was now 1979. The numbing cold of the January evening stung our faces as we walked out of our hotel and hurried across New York's Seventh Avenue toward the new Madison Square Garden.

It reminded me of another winter long before, the winter of my fiery terror. The memory passed through me at a depth I barely perceived. My wife's hand was tucked tightly inside my arm, her head down and close to my shoulder to ward off the cold. I could feel the chill nip at my ankles as we began the walk up to the Garden entrance. Wordlessly we walked, our silence indicating our preoccupation with just getting inside where it was warm.

Once inside, we went to the appropriate gate; I showed our passes, and we received instructions on how to reach the section assigned to us. As we walked along the corridor leading to our seats, Ruth voiced our feelings: "It's been a long time since we were able to be together like this, Glenn, away from home, just the two of us. It's been a good four days. But I'll be glad to get home tomorrow."

"Me, too."

It had been a great four days. But that night, January 20, 1979, our feelings were mixed. The reason for being at the Garden was nostalgically overshadowed by what we'd left behind.

"It's just another award," I said.

"It's not 'just another award,' Glenn Cunningham. That's what you always say. Being named athlete of the century is a lot more than 'just another award.'" Ruth's hand closed tightly about my arm.

"Well, it's not really 'athlete of the century,' Ruth. Something like 'outstanding track performer of the century.'"

"Even so, it's great they recognize you like this. Maybe some of the publicity will help the kids."

The kids. What about those youngsters who had stayed with us during the past thirty years? Some of them were middle-aged by now! Were their lives at all different because of the experience?

And Ruth. She had gone through many tough times brought on by my mistakes and stubbornness. And our ten children—how great they had been to share their parents with so many other kids.

"Here we are," she announced, glancing at the tickets to match the numbers with the seats. "Are you supposed to go down to the front?"

"I don't know." I glanced down at the oval track. Television cameras and crew members cluttered the area.

"I think you are, Glenn. Why don't you go ahead, and I'll sit here and wait for you?"

As I walked down the steps leading to the middle of the track area, my thoughts continued to dwell on Arkansas, our home now.

I had to face the reality that I couldn't do the things I used to. I was nearly seventy years old. But I wondered, *Is there still time to do more?* The opportunities were there; many troubled youths struggle to become adults in a world that often treats them with cruelty and hardship.

"You're Glenn Cunningham, aren't you?" The voice was pleasant and brought me back to the reality of the moment. The young man with a badge was apparently in charge of the awards ceremony. "We'll be ready for you in a little while. Why don't you make yourself comfortable? Sit right here, and we'll let you know when we're ready."

"Thank you." I made my way over camera cables and around crew members to a small group of chairs nearby. The races had begun and would continue throughout the evening. The awards would come later.

I was suddenly struck by the irony of it all. Here I was about to receive an award as the outstanding track performer in Madison Square Garden's hundred-year history. Yet my performance in the more important and truly meaningful things of life had been spotty.

There had been many times when I had wanted to quit both running and our youth work but had struggled back from adversity instead. It had become habitual, continuing to struggle, trying just a little harder, and then making it. Only I hadn't always made it. Why had it taken me so long to discover the reason?

Now, after the discovery, my time was running out. *Things could have been so different*, I reminded myself.

Absently, I began paging through the program. Athletes young enough to be my grandsons were sprinting and running their way through the competition that surged around the track. It brought back so many memories.

How many times had I raced under circumstances similar to these? The familiar glare of the overhead lights, bathing the track in a brilliance rivaling the sun; the *pat-pat* of mixed rhythms as runners rounded the curve and went into the stretch; the gentle murmurs of the crowd erupting into a roar as an especially exciting race neared its end. It started my adrenaline flowing.

The young man in charge of the arrangements came over again. "It'll be about another hour, Dr. Cunningham." I smiled and continued looking at the program. On page 46 was the citation "Glenn Cunningham, the dominant mile and 1500-meter runner of the 1930s, has been selected as the outstanding track performer of the century of Madison Square Garden's history."*

* Editor's note: In that eight-season span (1933–1940), Cunningham, a product of the University of Kansas, raced in thirty-one Garden mile or 1500-meter races and won twenty-one of them. In these distances, he established six world records. Cunningham is credited correctly with making the mile the glamour event in indoor track.

So many obstacles had marred the road to this award. From that little country school on the Kansas prairie where my life had nearly ended in an inferno of terror and pain to college track meets, the difficult races in the Olympics, and the youth work, something had always seemed to be there that needed overcoming.

After the ceremony, Ruth and I walked back to our hotel room, not minding the cold so much now after the presentation's warmth and the crowd.

"What were you thinking about, Glenn, when they gave you that award?"

I was silent for a moment, wondering how to answer. "I thought about all the obstacles."

"Like the fire that burned your legs so bad?"

"Yes, that. And the youngsters."

"Which ones?"

"Well, all of 'em." I laughed, remembering. "Kids too sick to run, but ran and won the race."

"Do you feel good about what you've done in seventy years, Glenn?"

"I gave it all I had."

"That's all an athlete can do, isn't it?"

I wrestled for a moment with that. "No, I don't think it is."

"Why?"

"Because during all those years, people just saw Glenn Cunningham. The efforts of one man. You know, and now I know, that this is never enough."

Ruth squeezed my arm. "What would you have done differently?"

"I was too much like my father: a disciplinarian, hard working, stubborn, and suspicious of churches. What's wrong with that is that we're never good enough on our own. We need that outside influence in our lives. I've always been a believer in God, but there were so many times when I could have taken a stand for Him and didn't. When I could have sought His help and didn't, to my loss."

"You wanted to do things on your own."

"That's right. And what hurts now is that we might have helped more youngsters where it counts, inside them, if I hadn't been so stubborn."

She took my hand and pressed it against her cheek.

"You've lived unselfishly, Glenn, never quitting on any person or difficulty. I prayed a long time ago that the Lord would give you a meaningful and fulfilled life. He answered that prayer magnificently, and He did it in a double dose because along the way, we both discovered Jesus Christ as the source of every provision in life. We have the opportunity to learn about Him. About His plan for our lives and sharing all of this with those youngsters who came our way."

I felt such sudden warmth inside me that I wanted to stop and hug Ruth right there on the sidewalks of New York City. She was right. Our prayers are answered in ways far greater than we could imagine. And through her prayers, I found that deep inner peace that I had been seeking when we met in 1946.

Over the years, I have learned that it is possible to accomplish many things at a human level through courage and persistence. But to gain that special inner satisfaction, we are dependent on God, who fulfills and enriches us beyond our wildest dreams.

Epilogue

Robert B. Gregg

On March 10, 1988, as he performed chores at his ranch, Glenn Cunningham passed away. The extraordinary man was seventy-eight years old. Newspapers around the world carried news of the legendary runner and educator.

During his life, he often said he would rather train a mediocre athlete with a great attitude than a talented athlete with a bad attitude. One of his favorite sayings was "Your attitude will make you or break you."

He wanted to be the best in life, even though he knew that failure was as important to success as winning. He exemplified the need to win honestly, aim high, pursue happiness, and never quit.

His most lasting monument, then and now, is not the awards or even the amazing story. His greatest tribute is over 8,400 children whose lives continue to show that when the race seems lost, the odds are overwhelming, and the pain becomes too much—never quit.

My Motivation

Central to human life is the pursuit of meaning, not the pursuit of happiness. We only invite frustration if we expect life to be primarily pleasurable. Life imposes obligations and responsibilities. Pleasure and happiness come from responding to the tasks of life. We ought to accept God's gift of joy and find happiness in living our lives content in a task. We all try to avoid pain, but we cannot always escape it. When we cannot avoid it, we should find meaning in it.

In this country, we look upon happiness and freedom from pain as inalienable rights. Our worship of pleasure feeds this. Christ warned us that in this life, there would be sorrow. Life has its ups and downs, its joys and pains, its pleasure and despair. If we look at life realistically, we know that suffering cannot be eliminated, but it must be faced truthfully. God's work done in God's way will receive God's supply. God does not promise that our faith will free us from all discouragement and conflict, but He does promise that the peace and power of the Holy Spirit will give us the kind of joy that enables us to weather any storm of affliction of the body, mind, and spirit. Christian joy is that quiet, inner contentment that results from "perfect acquiescence to God's will."

Often we consider suffering to be the same as defeat. Depression cannot be eliminated, but it can be handled constructively.*

Often depression hits us just before the Lord gives us a greater blessing, such as success or achievement amid a long stretch of unbroken labor. God allows depression and pain as instruments of growth and effectiveness. "Not by might, nor by power, but by my Spirit, saith

* The wisdom to inspire others comes only to those who suffer sorrow and are acquainted with grief.

the Lord" (Zach 4:6). The presence of God is the joy of His people, but any suspicions of His absence are distracting beyond measure, an insurmountable mountain that no one would be able to climb. God can make His sons of thunder anywhere, but he can make His Barnabas only in the fire.

Never ridicule a nervous and hypocritical person. God never placed Joseph in the pit without drawing him up again to fill the throne. It is good for me to have been afflicted so that I might know how to speak a word of encouragement to one who is weary, depressed, or wounded.

Glenn Cunningham